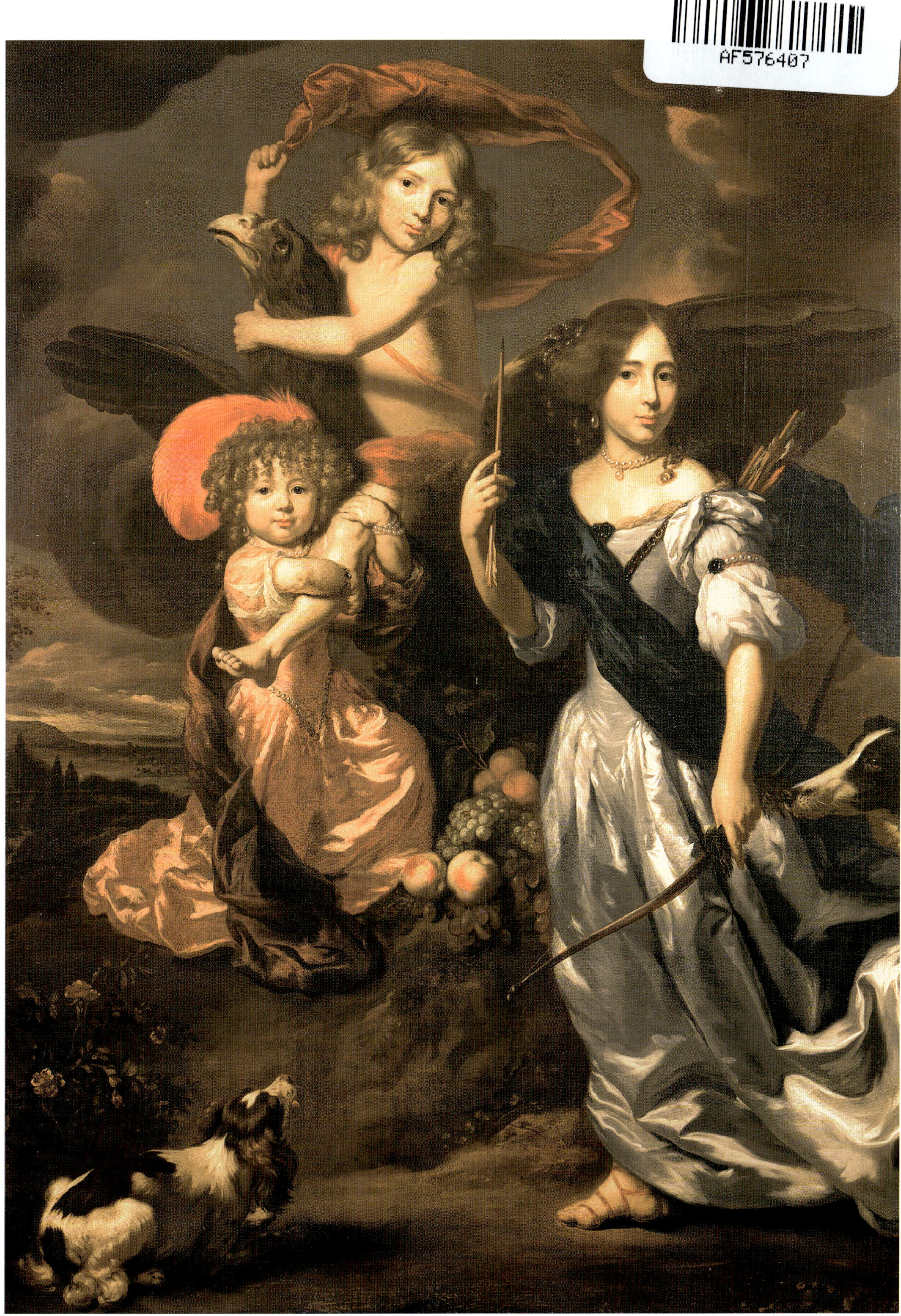

Children in Art

A Century of Change

Curtis L. Carter

WITH ESSAYS BY

Anne Higonnet

James Marten

Published by the
Patrick and Beatrice Haggerty Museum of Art
Marquette University, Milwaukee, Wisconsin

Children in Art: A Century of Change
February 12-May 23, 1999

Organized by the Patrick and Beatrice Haggerty Museum of Art, Marquette University

Photographs:
Cat. nos. 1, 10, 16, 19, 31, 36, 51, 52, 54, photographs by Murray Weiss
Cat. no. 3, Henry Art Gallery, University of Washington-Seattle, photograph by Richard Nicol
Cat. nos. 13, 47, 48, Milwaukee Art Museum, photographs by Larry Sanders
Cat. no. 25, Brooklyn Museum of Art
Cat. no. 32, Milwaukee Art Museum, photograph by P. Richard Eells
Cat. no. 34, © 1999 Artists Rights Society (ARS), New York/VG Bild-Kunst, Bonn; Milwaukee Art Museum, photograph by Larry Sanders
Page 10: Philipp Otto Runge, *The Hülsenbeck Children (Die Hülsenbeckschen Kinder),* 1805-06, oil on canvas, 51 3/4 x 56 1/2 in., Hamburger Kunsthalle; photograph copyright Elke Walford
Page 29: Timothy Cummings, *Children with Dead Bird,* 1997, acrylic on wood, 17 x 16 in., Collection of Gary Noguera and Courtesy Catharine Clark Gallery, San Francisco, California
Page 30: James Rosenquist, *Growth Plan,* 1966, 70 x 140 1/4 in., Courtesy Iwaki City Art Museum, Japan

International Standard Book Number: 0-945366-06-X
Library of Congress Catalog Card Number: 98-83162

Catalogue designed by Paula Schulze
Catalogue printed by Zimmermann Printing Company

Catalogue printed on Potlatch McCoy Silk Cover, Basis 120 lb.
and Potlatch McCoy Velour Text, Basis 100 lb.

Cover: Mary Cassatt, *Baby John Asleep, Sucking His Thumb,* c. 1910 (cat. no. 9)
Page 1: Nicolas Maes, *Mythological Subject,* 1673 (cat. no. 31)

Contents

Preface

The subject of children in art is represented throughout the history of western art. Our research for *Children in Art: A Century of Change* produced an endless repertory of children's images by artists in virtually every representational style and era. In responding to our requests for works for the exhibition, several museums noted that the pictures requested were among their most popular images with visitors and were central to their educational programs. Notwithstanding the impression that children in art might only be a trivial or sentimental topic for academic art history, there is a sustained and growing interest in the subject. During the past twenty years, numerous works on children in art have appeared. These include studies of images in mainstream art history, folk art, and photography, as well as advertising and illustration. Among recent scholarly publications are the following: *Children in America*, 1979 (High Museum of Art); Anita Schorsch, *Images of Childhood: An Illustrated Social History,* 1979 (with pictures and commentary on family, child labor, education, and related topics); Sandra Brandt and Elissa Cullman, *Small Folk: A Celebration of Childhood in America,* 1980 (Museum of American Folk Art; a study of children in folk art from the seventeenth to the nineteenth centuries); *Angels and Urchins,* 1980 (Joslyn Museum); Sara Holdsworth and Joan Crossley, *Innocence and Experience: Images of Children in British Art from 1600 to the Present,* 1992 (Manchester [England] City Art Galleries); Robert Rosenblum, *The Romantic Child: From Runge to Sendak,* 1988; Werner Spies, *Picasso's World of Children*, 1994 (a study of Picasso's uses of childhood in his art, the child as symbol, etc.); Jonathan Fineberg, *The Innocent Eye: Children's Art and the Modern Era,* 1997 (a study of the influences of children's art on modern art); Anne Higonnet, *Pictures of Innocence: The History and Crisis of Ideal Childhood,* 1998; and *Ashcan Kids,* 1998 (Berry Hill Galleries, New York; children in the art of Henri, Luks, Glackens, Bellows, and Sloan). These books and exhibition catalogues offer a variety of historical and contemporary approaches to the subject.

Given the immense output of images of children by artists, there are many omissions in the exhibition. Particularly notable is the lack of works by Picasso, whose portrayals of children (both images of his own children and the impersonal pictures) are among the most insightful, and Balthus, whose images of children also raise important questions concerning the representation of children in art. Nevertheless, the works available in the exhibition will offer viewers a broad range of insight into the creative energy devoted to the subject of children in art and hopefully cause them to think in new ways about the subject.

Curtis L. Carter
Director

Acknowledgments

Children in Art: A Century of Change has provided the opportunity to explore a theme of considerable interest and importance. The effort has benefited from the cooperation of many friends of the Haggerty Museum, private and institutional lenders, the Museum staff, and the anonymous benefactors who provided exhibition funding. The initial idea for the exhibition emerged from conversations with David and Catherine Straz, whose enthusiasm for paintings featuring children encouraged me to pursue an exhibition on the subject. Lillian Rojtman Berkman, president of the Rojtman Foundation, Frances Beatty of Richard L. Feigen and Co., Holly Solomon of Holly Solomon Gallery, M. P. Naud of Hirschl and Adler Galleries, and Edward Wilson of the Fund for Fine Arts provided useful leads on artists whose repertory included children. Dean Sobel of the Milwaukee Art Museum, Barbara Dayer Gallati of the Brooklyn Museum of Art, Marsha V. Gallagher of the Joslyn Art Museum, and Richard Andrews of the Henry Art Gallery, University of Washington all were helpful in accommodating requests for loans. I would like to thank Anne Higonnet, associate professor of art history at Wellesley College, and James Marten, associate professor of history at Marquette University, for providing thought-provoking essays for the catalogue. Both have recently published books on the cultural understanding of children. George Dimock, assistant professor of art history, University of North Carolina at Greensboro; Jonathan Fineberg, professor of art history, University of Illinois at Urbana-Champaign; and Milwaukee psychiatrist Anthony Meyer have provided their insights on children in art for exhibition-related lectures and workshops.

The Haggerty Museum staff contributed substantially to all aspects of the exhibition and catalogue. Lee Coppernoll arranged exhibition-related events and coordinated educational programs; Paula Schulze edited and designed the catalogue and assisted with installation; Steven Anderson, assisted by Tim Dykes, designed and installed the exhibition; James Kieselburg organized loans and arranged shipping and insurance; Stephanie Bjork coordinated publicity and assisted with research; Joyce Ashley and Nicole Hauser provided administrative support; student assistants Juan Ramos and Lisa Neumaier helped with the preparation of the catalogue; and Clayton Montez coordinated security. Their team effort warrants high praise.

Finally, thanks are due to all of the lenders. Without their generosity and cooperation the exhibition would not have been possible:

C. L. C.

Lenders to the Exhibition

Artemis Fine Arts, Inc., New York
Autry Museum of Western Heritage, Los Angeles
David Barnett Gallery, Milwaukee
Brooklyn Museum of Art
Jean Carter, Milwaukee
Marvin and Janet Fishman, Milwaukee
Dr. and Mrs. Milton F. Gutglass, Milwaukee
Henry Art Gallery, University of Washington-Seattle
Hirschl and Adler Galleries, New York
Joslyn Art Museum, Omaha, Nebraska
Kevin and Margaret Kinney, Milwaukee
Milwaukee Art Museum
Dr. and Mrs. Robert S. Pavlic, Brookfield
Private Collection
Private Collection, Switzerland
The Rojtman Foundation, New York
Rosenthal and Rosenthal, Inc., New York
Schiller and Bodo European Paintings, New York
Mr. and Mrs. Ted Slavin, Los Angeles
Catherine and David A. Straz, Jr., Milwaukee
Edward Wilson, Fund for Fine Arts, Chevy Chase, Maryland

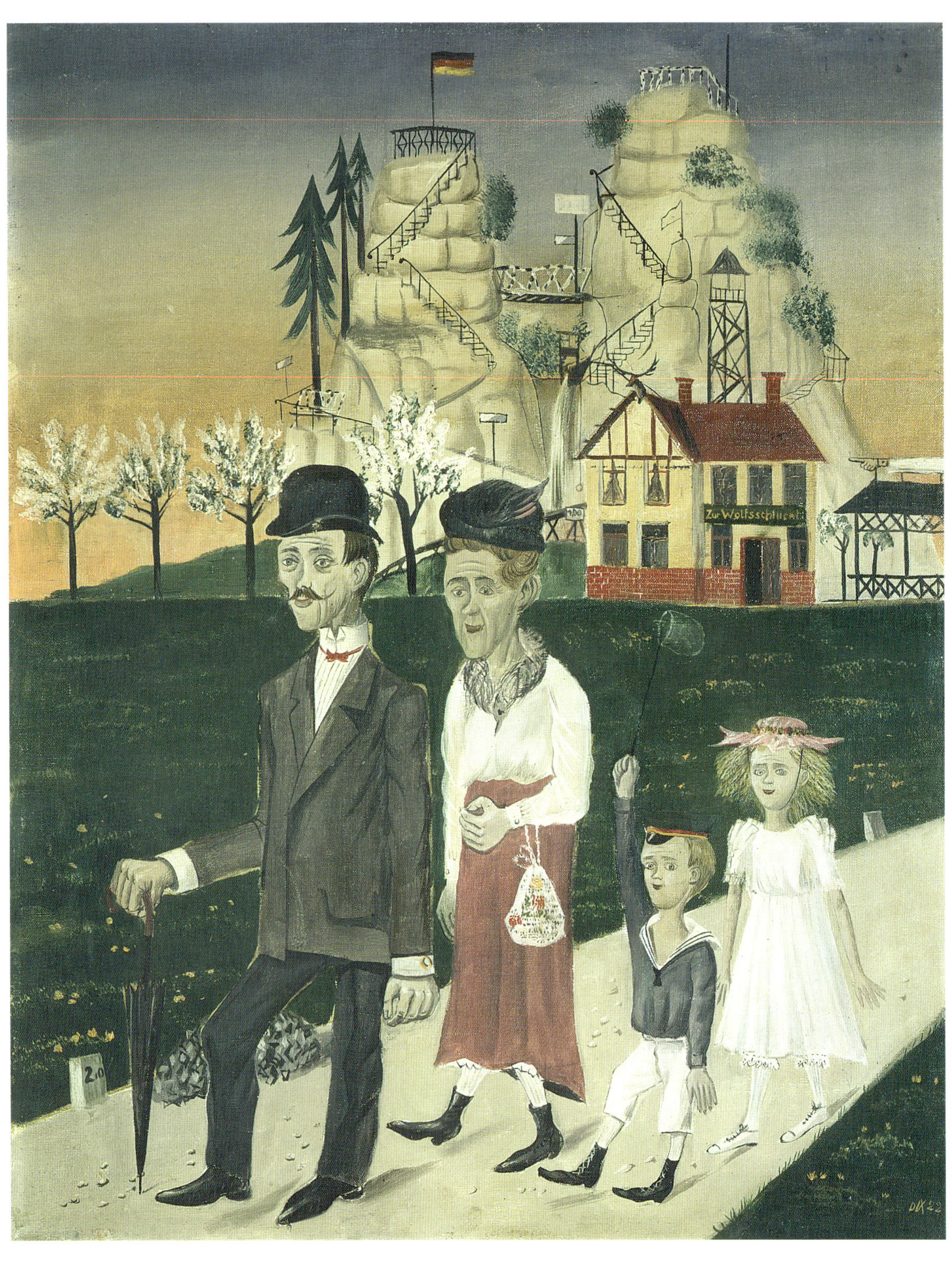

Otto Dix
Sunday Outing (Sonntagsspaziergang), 1922
(cat. no. 14)

Paradise Lost?
Changing Images of Childhood

CURTIS L. CARTER

The focus of *Children in Art: A Century of Change* is on American and European representations of children from the mid-nineteenth to mid-twentieth centuries. With respect to artists' depictions of children, this particular time period embraces the concepts of Romantic innocence (introduced in the eighteenth century and advanced in the nineteenth century), Realism, Impressionism, Modernist formalism, *Neue Sachlichkeit* ("New Objectivity"), and social realism of the mid-twentieth century. The exhibition documents the major changes in societal attitudes toward children during a century when children were at times seen as miniature adults useful for their contributions to the labor force, as symbols of Romantic innocence and purity, as victims of societal and personal abuse, and as objects of loving care and also desire. This is a century in which specialists and the public have become skeptical of Romantic innocence in images of children because of concerns over implicit and explicit childhood sexuality reflected in the works of artists past and present.

Seventeenth-century Puritan ideas concerning children were dominated by the notion of the child as a miniature adult beset by evil and in need of redemption through work and religious faith. Cotton Mather's condemnation of children's idleness and play, and his invocation of the virtues of diligence and work, typify an era in American and European life.[1] These sentiments were sometimes concealed behind mythological representations as in Nicolas Maes's *Mythological Subject,* 1673 (cat. no. 31, p. 1). In this work, the children are represented as Diana the huntress, the young Phyrgian shepherd Ganymede, and Ceres, the goddess of plenty. During the eighteenth century, the dominant cultural ideas governing the representation of children in art underwent significant change toward a Romantic idealized notion of children as the embodiment of innocence. Innocence in this context suggests a range of possible meanings. It might refer to naturalness, purity, simplicity, guilelessness, inexperience, playfulness, or to a state of being unfettered by evil and free of sexual intent or understanding.

The change from earlier views of childhood was influenced in part by the Enlightenment philosophers John Locke and Jean-Jacques Rousseau, who viewed childhood as a distinct stage of human development that determined the moral and psychological person in adulthood. In *Some Thoughts Concerning Education,* Locke recommended that the natural qualities of children govern their training, including the elements of play, high spirits, and gamesome humor.[2] Rousseau also recognized childhood as a special state of human development with its own ways of seeing, thinking, and being, which required an education sensitive to these conditions.[3] Rousseau advocated that, instead of turning them over to servants and boarding schools, parents should care for and direct the socialization of their own children. As a result of such influences, the concept of children and family in aristocratic Europe changed radically from a previous era in which children were often regarded indifferently by parents. In previous times, pain and confinement resulting from childbirth tended to overshadow the joys of children for their mothers, and the relationship of children to fathers was often formal and distant. In the upper levels of society, children had been regarded as instruments for transferring property and as burdens to be relegated for their upbringing to servants and private schoolmasters. At the opposite end of society, children were valued for their contributions to the agrarian and the evolving industrial labor markets.

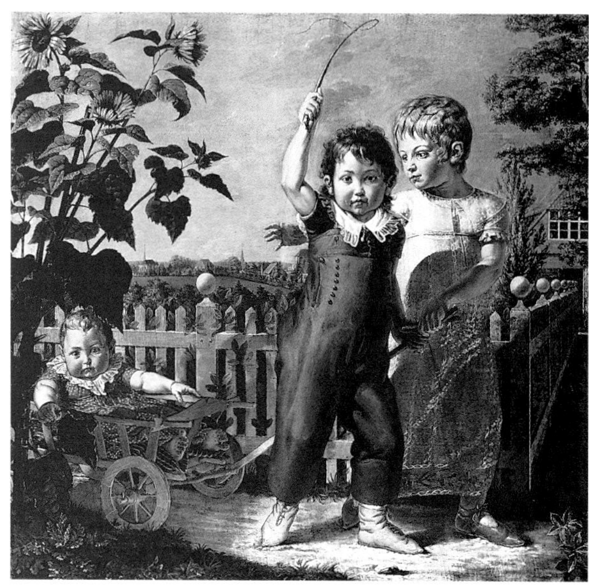

Philip Otto Runge, *The Hülsenbeck Children (Die Hülsenbeckschen Kinder),* 1805-06

The Romantic view of childhood has been advanced in art history by Robert Rosenblum in a study of Philipp Otto Runge's children,[4] in Carol Duncan's "Happy Mothers and Other New Ideas in French Art,"[5] and by other studies of children in art. Most recently, it has been critically examined in Anne Higonnet's book *Pictures of Innocence.*[6] Rosenblum found in Runge's depictions of children a kind of primal natural innocence and a link between childhood and the vital, magical energies of nature. In both a portrait of his son, *Otto Sigismund in a Highchair,* 1805 (Rosenblum, plate 19), and in *The Hülsenbeck Children,* 1805-06 (above), Runge's pictures reveal a mysterious world scaled to childhood and provide a distinctive child's perspective. The Romantic vision of childhood exemplified in Runge's paintings began in the eighteenth century and was disbursed through the works of various artists working throughout the nineteenth century.[7] It persists into the twentieth century in various expressions in the fine arts and in the popular culture of illustrations and photography.

Higonnet contrasts the concept of the innocent Romantic child in art with her own view that pictures in the late twentieth century feature "knowing children" whose sexual awareness must be taken into account in their interpretation. In Higonnet's analysis, Joshua Reynold's painting, *The Age of Innocence,* c. 1788, a portrait of his great-niece Offy, exemplifies the features of Romantic innocence. According to Higonnet,

> The Romantic child makes a good show of having no class, no gender, and no thoughts—of being socially, sexually, and psychically innocent. . . .
> . . . According to Romantic pictures of children, innocence must be an edenic state from which adults fall, never to return. Nor can Romantic children know adults; they are by definition unconscious of adult desires, including adults' desires for childhood.[8]

The situation with respect to children has always been more complex than a Romantic account of childhood might suggest. Children of working-class families did not normally participate in the idealized Romantic model of childhood.[9] Rather, their lives would have been depicted as grounded in the activities of daily life, and their destinies were forged through their early entry into apprenticeships or into the agrarian and industrial labor forces, where they often performed under dangerous working conditions and were vulnerable to exploitation. Here, in the context of a laissez-faire economy with no system of public education, working-class children were often viewed as a profitable source of labor.[10]

> The evils of child labor in England and America were first made obvious in the cotton mills that frequently employed children as young as four years old. . . . A child over seven worked from sunrise to sunset six days a week with two and a half days off a year. . . . But as bad as was the state of the working child in industry, he was even worse off in the homes and workshops of private families. Thousands of children were actually sold by their parents as slaves to chimney sweeps, mine owners, and other employers.[11]

On the other hand, work provided protection, independence, and the possibility of education. The alternatives for working-class children were not all that attractive.

> A child out of work—especially a boy child and, even more frightening, a *poor* boy child—threatened the peace of the streets. And it was commonly believed that children of artisan and laboring families without work would be doomed to a future of vagrancy and jail.[12]

While such conditions continued, at least through the nineteenth century, laws regulating child labor and prescribing compulsory education, and public institutions, including orphanages and schools, provided increased protection for working children. At their best, however, the experiences of poor children were not likely to produce the idealized childhood. To the extent that it existed in reality at all, Romantic innocence would remain a privilege of the upper classes.

Toward the end of the nineteenth century, and during the early years of the twentieth century, romanticized images were supplanted in part by newer approaches to the representation of childhood. With the emergence of Modern art in the late nineteenth century, artists were increasingly attentive to formalist issues in art, including new approaches to painting styles, and concern with the elements of color, space, and the medium itself. While artists continued to paint children, their interest in the subject became subordinate to the processes of art making. This did not mean necessarily an abandonment of societal concerns even among those who chose to concentrate on the formalist issues. Among the alternatives to formalism were the starkly realistic *Neue Sachlichkeit* images of children which documented the effects of war and urban poverty on children in post-war Europe. In this context, children's images function as a form of social commentary, thus mirroring the adverse social and economic travails of children in a changing society. Moreover, the Dadaists, in the early years from 1913 to 1924, who attempted to confront the status quo of bourgeois society as well as to undo traditional practices in art, and the social realist painters of the 1930s and 1940s, especially in the United States, continued to address social concerns.

With the emergence in the late twentieth century of neo-Puritan attitudes toward the representation of sexuality in art, uneasiness over representations of children that might involve sexual content has become an issue in how we look at fine art paintings as well as photography, illustration, and advertising. The writings of Simone de Beauvoir and, more recently, James Kincaid on the sexuality of children have undercut nineteenth-century assumptions concerning childhood innocence.[13] The recognition of children as knowing objects of desire in the paintings of certain artists from William Adolphe Bouguereau on, and in the photography of artists such as Sally Mann and Larry Clark, presents a need to rethink innocence in the images of childhood past and present.[14] Accordingly, the images of Bouguereau (cat. no. 3) and William Sargeant Kendall (cat. no. 25) might well lose immunity from scrutiny with the loss of the concept of childhood innocence and the breakdown of assumptions concerning a radical separation of childhood from adulthood. Although interest in laws concerning pornography in art has intensified in recent times, so far such paintings have not prompted raids on museums. The concern over childhood sexuality is but one of a number of issues involving the representation of children and their place in contemporary society. This issue and others concerning childhood identity, children's experiences of death, child neglect and abuse, and increasing violence among children, have generated a new wave of research on all aspects of childhood and call for a rethinking of ideas concerning childhood that emerged apart from the Romantic ideal.[15]

The Haggerty Exhibition

The scope of *Children in Art: A Century of Change* encompasses American, English, French, and German genre paintings; Impressionist, Post-Impressionist and Expressionist works, as well as other forms of Modern art; and social realism. It offers a significant representation of children as seen by the *Neue Sachlichkeit* artists working in Germany during the 1920s. These works, which reveal the darker aspects of society's treatment of children, show the conditions of need experienced by children between the two world wars in Europe. They are symbolic of aspects of childhood that are masked in the tradition of Romantic innocence inherited from the nineteenth century. Private collections such as the Rojtman Foundation collection, the Marvin and Janet Fishman collection of German art of the 1920s, and the Catherine and David A. Straz, Jr. collection of Impressionist art, as well as the Milwaukee Art Museum, the Joslyn Art Museum, the Brooklyn Museum of Art, the Henry Art Gallery, the Haggerty Museum, and other galleries and collections provided works for the exhibition.

Romantic Innocence in Nineteenth-Century Genre Paintings

The earliest works in the exhibition are genre paintings from c. 1840 to 1870. They include representations of the children of Romantic innocence and various genre scenes. Alfred De Dreux's *Innocence between Two Thieves,* c. 1859 and John Mix Stanley's *Young Chief Uncas* offer contrasting European and American representations of Romantic innocence (cat. nos. 12, 50; pp. 57, 58). De Dreux was a court painter under King Louis Philippe and served Emperor Napoleon III during the Second Empire. His painting depicts a young girl seated with unquestioning trust on a large mastiff. To the left, a black spaniel sits positioned on hind legs. In the background are mountains and sky. Between the dogs and in the idyllic setting, the young girl in hat and fancy dress, with stylish buttoned shoes, exemplifies the essence of aristocratic Romantic innocence. Her innocent demeanor is reinforced by the action of her canine companions, who eye the crust of bread held in her hand with less than innocent intent. Stanley provides an image of a young boy chief dressed in tribal feathered headdress, beadwork necklaces, leather garment, and moccasins, holding a tomahawk in his right hand. The little chief is seated high above the plain on a rock and surrounded only by the natural hills and sky of the western United States. Both

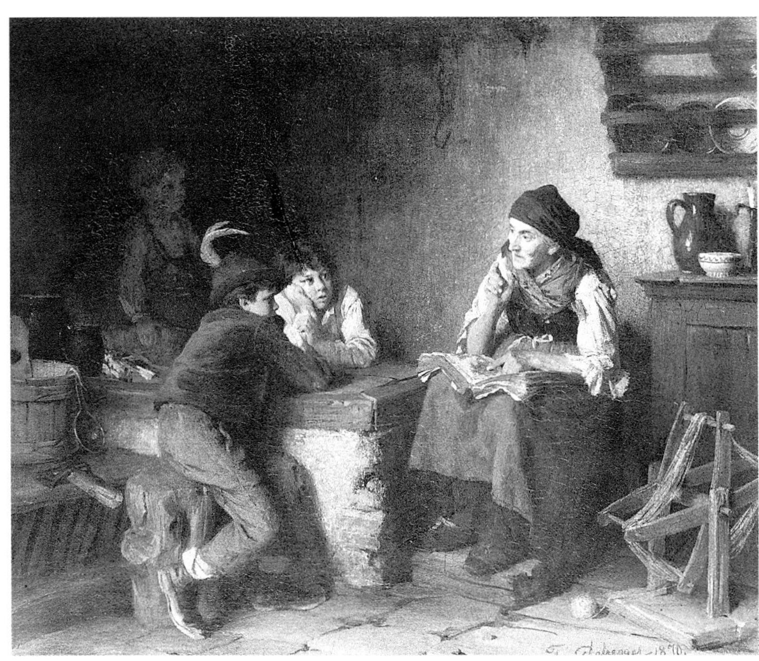

Franz von Defregger
The Story Teller, 1870
(cat. no. 13)

the young European girl and the Native-American boy are symbols of Romantic innocence, free of corruption, in harmony with nature, yet not without connections to the cultures that they represent. Their costumes link each figure to a world with complex and longstanding cultural traditions, the one associated with the European aristocracy, the other with an American tribal culture with close ties to the open spaces of nature.

Most of the other works from this era show children lovingly depicted in an idealized setting. For instance, *The Young Artist*, 1840 (cat. no. 7, p. 58) by Thomas Mickell Burnham shows a young child in his backyard sketching a boy of African descent wearing a red hat. The black child, the young artist, and three other children who observe the scene are all smiling. A grandmotherly figure watches approvingly from inside the doorway. The only notable differences between the participants is that the black boy is holding a shovel, thus identifying his role with work, while the others, apart from the artist, appear to be at leisure.

The remaining paintings from this time period show children with family or engaged in solo activities, still lovingly depicted in idealized settings. Johann Georg Meyer's *Girl with Knitting*, 1846 (cat. no. 32, p. 53) shows a young girl with braided hair engaged in the act of knitting. Framed in a rustic doorway with branches above her head, the girl gazes directly at the viewer. The romanticized innocence of childhood is exemplified in this work of a master painter of the golden age of Düsseldorf. Franz von Defregger draws upon folk history for the subject of *The Story Teller*, 1870 (cat. no. 13) which shows two young boys listening with full attention to the narrator of a tale. Two paintings by Pierre

Édouard Frère, who worked in France and was one of the most successful European painters of children, *Young Admiral,* c. 1860 and *Playing Mother*, 1865 (cat. nos. 17, 18; p. 59) continue in a romanticized mode of depicting children.[16] *Young Admiral*, set in a well-appointed nineteenth-century kitchen, shows a young boy clinging to the rim of a large wooden tub, gazing intently at his boat floating on the surface of the water within. The light from a nearby window shines on his angelic face. In *Playing Mother*, a young peasant girl in a large parlor chair is seen kissing the doll held closely on her lap. Her pose simulates a familiar art-historical theme of mother and child, which recurs frequently in Romantic portrayals.

Andrew W. Warren's *Clay Modeling*, c. 1866 (cat. no. 56, p. 59) features a young boy in an interior setting crafting a dog's head out of clay. In contrast to this genteel effort, a working boy in John George Brown's *Eating the Profits*, 1878 (cat. no. 4, p. 60) is enterprisingly positioned on the street awaiting customers for his apples and shoeshine business. At the moment, while business is slow, he consumes a portion of the apples. Brown is well known for making appealing portraits; his paintings tend to present children, even those in challenging circumstances, in an optimistic light.

Genre paintings featuring children continue during the period of 1870 to 1900, but with increasing competition from Academic Realism and Impressionism. In contrast to the previous examples, Edwin Howland Blashfield captures the isolation and frustration of childhood in *Waterloo: Total Defeat*, 1882 (cat. no. 2, p. 59). The child in this painting resides in a plush house with fine furniture, silver, artworks, and servants. None of these amenities conceal his unhappiness when his game of soldiers is interrupted by intruding adults about to sequester him in the nursery in order to set the table for dinner.[17]

A growing interest of the period in education is reflected in *The Dame's School*, c. 1900 (cat. no. 41, p. 43) by Walter Dendy Sadler and also in Eyre Crowe's *Boys of Blue Coat School*, 1877 (cat. no. 11, p. 60). Sadler takes the viewer inside an English dame school where the teacher, switches in hand, instructs five young Englishmen standing around a large globe. The instructor's physical height and stern countenance set her apart from the well-dressed upperclass students, whose somber gazes reflect attitudes from interested curiosity to pained endurance. *Boys of Blue Coat School* shows students actively engaged in independent learning, possibly at the Royal Hospital School now located at Greenwich. Here two boys in school uniform are intently involved with a microscope while a third gazes intently at his watch and two others look on. Not all education takes place in school, as John George Brown's *The Card Trick*, c. 1880s (cat. no. 5, p. 60) shows. Here, at curbside, a young black boy instructs his three companions—judging by their dress, boys of the street—in the artistry of card tricks. This teacher, unlike the one at the English dame school, delights his students who obviously take great pleasure in the lesson.

Mother and Child

Undoubtedly the most celebrated children's theme is the mother and child, well known throughout art history as Madonna and Child. The painters represented in the exhibition focus upon secularized representations of the mother and child which generally regard the child as a loving object for which maternal nurture is to be provided. We have already encountered this theme in Frère's *Playing Mother.* Another variation occurs in Frederick Waugh's *The Artist's Family at Home*, 1887 (cat. no. 57, p. 61). Here the mother is seated on a rocker playing with a baby held at arm's length, while her observing daughter imitates her by holding her doll in a similar pose. In contrast to this animated interactive mother-child image, Jozef Israëls, who drew inspiration from Rembrandt and from his own observations of daily life, provides a quiet interior scene with a seated mother keeping watch as her infant sleeps in a crib in front of a fireplace (*Dutch Interior,* c. 1898; cat. no. 24, p. 35). "Motherly kindness and idyllic sweetness" are manifest toward the sleeping child.[18]

Mary Cassatt, the only American to exhibit with the Impressionists in Paris, and arguably the most famous of all women artists in any age, chose to make the theme of mother and child her specialty after 1880 when her nieces and nephews came to live in Paris. Two works by Cassatt are included in the exhibition: *Peasant Mother and Child*, c. 1894 (cat. no. 8, p. 62), a rare drypoint and hand-colored aquatint, and *Baby John Asleep, Sucking His Thumb*, c. 1910 (cat. no. 9, p. 62), a pastel drawing.[19] The first shows a mother holding in her arms a child dressed in night clothes. The mother's head is in profile as she focuses lovingly on the closely held child, who reciprocates her affection and appears secure in the relationship. *Baby John Asleep, Sucking His Thumb* is executed in pastel, Cassatt's chosen medium for rendering mother-child images, and represents her fully developed Impressionist style. In this image, the mother is seated, facing forward, and the nude child rests against her body with his head on her left shoulder. The bright pastel strokes in blues, yellows, reds, and flesh tones against an indistinct background produce a highly sensuous surface that exemplifies both the idealization of childhood and its dissolution into the sensuality of the mother-child relationship. The sense of an idealized mother-child relationship thus rises to its highest moments in Cassatt's images.

Anne Higonnet contends that Cassatt looks at children's bodies as erotic objects. "Clothed or not, Cassatt's children represent the physical pleasure women and children give each other," which includes visual pleasure as well as the pleasures of touch.[20] Judith Barter argues, "In Cassatt's work, child nudity is not sexual but natural and sensual, symbolizing goodness." According to Barter, Cassatt is the only one of the French Impressionist painters to depict nude children.[21] By way of contrast, in Renoir's *Mother and Child*, 1881 (Barnes Collection), the child is fully clothed and seated on the mother's lap, reflecting the artist's scrupulous observation of domestic proprieties.[22]

By the end of the nineteenth century, and into the twentieth, variations in the ways of representing mother and child assume many forms. At one extreme is Norbert Goeneutte's *Reine Goeneutte Washing the Young Jean Geurard in the Artist's Studio*, 1889 (cat. no. 20, p. 61), a decidedly modern rendering of a mother washing her nude male child who appears to be six or seven years of age. The child sits on a chaise in the artist's studio; his mother is seated in front of him with a large copper wash bowl and sponge in the act of washing his body. There is no hint of overt erotic intent in the picture; yet the repercussions of late-twentieth-century discussions of sexuality in artistic representations of children require rethinking the interpretation of such pictures.

Another direction, toward formalism in the depiction of children, is indicated in Milton Avery's *Maternity*, 1933 (cat. no. 1, p. 63). This exquisite painting, which depicts Avery's wife and their child born in the midst of the Depression, is in a modernist style which is at the edge of figuration and abstraction. Its boldness is in its formal elements of color and shape, rather than its subject— the mother embracing the child who is wrapped in a brightly colored blanket. The baby's pink face tells the viewer that the baby is the focus of the picture. Nevertheless, the painting reveals a warmth and tenderness in the relation of mother and child. Avery was aware of the expressive dimensions and the political and social concerns of his time, but he translates his feelings on these matters into a subtle pictorial language of color and shape in the overall composition and scale of his works instead of through overtly expressive theatrical gestures or stormy landscapes.[23] His trademark ability to harmonize unexpected color combinations is reflected here in the blend of pinks and darker earth tones. Although decidedly modern, Avery sometimes invokes the simplicity found in the conventions of naïve or untrained artists, as he does in this picture.

The mother and child image in Jacques Villon's *Maternity*, c. 1948 (cat. no. 53, p. 84) carries the process of modern abstraction a step further. *Maternity* exemplifies the artist's interest in geometry, proportion, the golden section, and color. The image is set in a grid of colors and lines which show the artist's inventive imagination, with the aid of Neo-Impressionist, Cubist, and Futurist influences. The grid provides architectonic support for the image of a mother seated on a chair with the child cradled on her lap. The luminous shapes of the figures are cast in vibrant pinks, yellows, and greens carefully placed across the fragmented planar surface. Although there is no direct reference to the traditional Madonna and Christ Child of Christian iconography, this is one of several pictures done by Villon in the late 1940s that touch upon religious themes.[24] Villon's concern with abstract pictorial means and the oblique reference to the historic Madonna and Child deflect any didactic reading of the picture for its social meaning. The subject of mother and child has become mainly an object for the painter's convenience.

Child Portraits

The exhibition also includes paintings with solo images of children. One of the earliest of these is Max Liebermann's *The Cobbler's Girl*, 1871 (cat. no. 30, p. 64). Its subject is a small girl, standing full length, dressed in the attire of a working child. The child appears shy and somewhat uncertain as she stands on the edge of her foot, one hand clutching her skirt, with a finger pressed lightly between her teeth. This picture has a social and psychological edge that is lacking in most of the genre pictures of the era and is expressive, while largely devoid of sentimentality or local color. There are hints of the future international Impressionist and Expressionist developments in Liebermann's style. Could this picture qualify as an attempt to portray Romantic innocence, but in the context of a working-class society? Perhaps. But there is more to be read into the situation. This child's uncertain demeanor and lower social standing point to a different involvement with her world, one tempered by work and possibly by hardship or abuse.

William Adolphe Bouguereau produced a substantial body of images of mothers and children, shepherdesses, and children playing. His market for such paintings was middle-class homes, including those in England and America. On one level, his portraits of children are paradigms of Romantic innocence, but his frankness in overtly sexualizing his images brings his children into the world of adult sensibility.[25] The smoothness of his superb technique creates an impression of viewing something real, or at least photographically real. His paintings *The Story Book*, previously *Innocence*, 1877 (Los Angeles County Museum of Art), *Rest in Harvest*, 1865 (Philbrook Museum of Art, Tulsa, plate 39 in Wissman) and *Child at Bath*, 1886 (cat. no. 3, p. 65) all reflect different aspects of childhood. In *The Story Book*, which might well serve as an ideal representation of childhood innocence, the child sits holding an open book and looks directly out at the viewer. The girl in *Rest in Harvest* is portrayed as reclining in a seductive manner in a harvest field. The seminude child pictured in *Child at Bath* would appear to be a prime candidate for the representation of Romantic innocence. It is unclear how Bouguereau's contemporaries regarded such pictures, but it seems likely that his intended middle-class audience did not share the concern that a late-twentieth-century audience might have over possible child abuse or exploitation in such representations of child sexuality.

William Sergeant Kendall's painting *A Statuette*, 1915 (cat. no. 25) raises similar issues as the child paintings of Bouguereau. Kendall's seminude child stands before a chair in a formal pose facing the viewer. Her upper body is shown nude, while the lower half is draped, except for a single foot that extends seductively from beneath the cloth. This painting was included in an exhibition organized by conceptual artist Joseph Kosuth with objects from the collection of the Brooklyn Museum, to promote public discussion and reflection on "unspeakable objects" in art.[26]

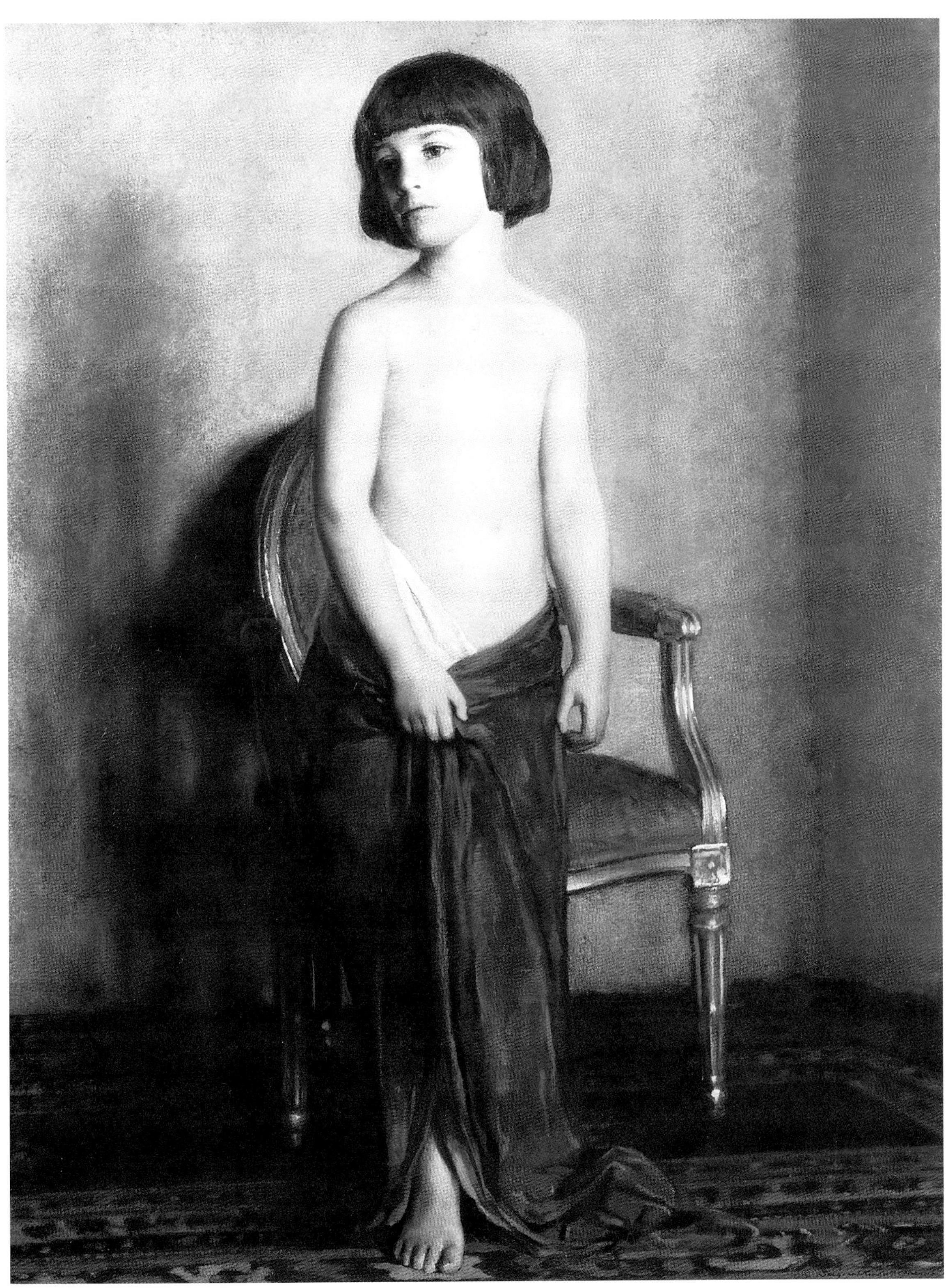

William Sergeant Kendall
A Statuette, 1915 (cat. no. 25)

Less controversial are the Impressionist and Post-Impressionist images of Berthe Morisot, Pierre-Auguste Renoir, and Édouard Vuillard. Morisot is known for her intimate portraits rendered with a certain spontaneity and naturalness and for her ability to capture the essence of a particular moment. *Julie Listening*, 1888 (cat. no. 33, p. 32), which pictures her daughter Julie Manet, and her niece Jeannie Gobillard (whose hands appear on the keys of the piano), symbolizes the close bond of maternity experienced between mother and daughter. Morisot viewed her art as an important means of recording her daughter's growth and as a teaching tool to transmit her own artistic heritage to the next generation.[27] This image is one of four oil sketches made in preparation for the final pastel version of 1888. In the painting, Julie gazes toward the artist (her mother) while her cousin Jeannie faces the music, thus symbolizing the bond between mother and daughter.[28]

Renoir's *Portrait of Coco*, 1902 (cat. no. 39, p. 67) is of his third son, Claude, also called Coco. The child is wearing an ivory-white yoked dress with full sleeves and pleated middle, and a ruffled hat with a large bow tied with ribbon beneath the chin. His right hand tightly grasps an indiscernible object, perhaps a flower. The face is rounded with cheeks and lips tinted red. In this charming painting, Renoir celebrates the joyous experience of seeing his son play and discover the world. The picture again represents an idealized childhood, whose joyfulness and beauty are revealed in the clarity and freshness of the artist's sensitive rendering. It is said that Claude was a favorite among Renoir's models. Throughout his career, Renoir painted many images of children in virtually all conventional poses: interior parlor scenes reminiscent of the genre paintings discussed earlier (*The Afternoon of the Children at Wargemont*, 1884, Nationalgalerie, Staatliche Museen, Berlin); mother and child (*Madam Renoir with Pierre*, 1886, Norton Simon Foundation, Los Angeles); as well as group portraits (*Two Little Circus Girls*, 1879, The Art Institute of Chicago); and solo portraits (*Girl with Falcon*, 1880, Sterling and Francis Clark Art Institute, Williamstown, Massachusetts).[29]

Édouard Vuillard's *Child with Ribbons*, c. 1904-05 (cat. no. 55, p. 66) is one of several paintings of children done by Vuillard throughout his career.[30] This picture shows a seminude child seated on the floor surrounded by a box with brightly colored ribbons and perhaps some painted sketches. Whether these items were provided with parental approval or obtained through independent discovery is unknown, but the happy child is engrossed in play and appears totally free from the cares of the adult world. The child in this image is rendered in a more naturalistic style than are Vuillard's earlier interiors. The image of childhood suggested in both the Renoir and the Vuillard pictures is of children who are loved, protected, and well cared for.

Neue Sachlichkeit Children

The strongest social statement found in the exhibition is seen in the *Neue Sachlichkeit* or "New Objectivity" pictures of children from the 1920s and 1930s in post-war Germany. Although the dominant feeling in these works is one of angst, whether expressed directly or through irony, the pictures cover a variety of situations involving children. Among the works represented is Otto Dix's *Sunday Outing*, 1922 (cat. no. 14, p. 8). One of the master works from this period featuring the bourgeois family, *Sunday Outing* is a satirical portrayal of a German family on a Sunday excursion, painted in a neo-naïve style. The family is arranged in a patriarchal order with the dominant father in the lead, and mother, son, and daughter respectively in subordinate positions. The father's high white collar signals a high-ranking professional such as a lawyer or a businessman. In the background are a small train station and twin mountain peaks where raw nature has been adapted for tourist outings. The irony of the depiction is enhanced by the artist's caricature of a naïve style of painting. Dix painted this work at a time when state policy dictated that support for family life and the propagation and social education of children was a central task of the state.[31] There is an illusion of innocence, reflected both in the neo-naïve style and in the attempt to sustain the purity of a bourgeois life style in the midst of social conditions that portent its end. The girl's white dress might also suggest that she is intended as a satire of Romantic innocence.

In contrast to the bourgeois family depicted in Dix's painting, Karl Völker's *Gypsy Family*, c. 1920 (cat. no. 54, p. 68) portrays the tragic drama of an incarcerated Romany (Gypsy) family. Family members are dressed in prison issue, the mother in red, the father in brown, and the child in blue. The three stand erect and with dignity, their bodies overlapping. The face of the mother expresses an air of defiance; the father's almost expressionless face nevertheless betrays his ultimate concern. But the terrified look on the face of the wide-eyed child clinging fearfully to his father's leg clearly tells the story of their impending doom. Here the child is represented as a victim of ethnic discrimination.

The only other picture in the exhibition from this era with parent and child as its subject is *A Woman of 1934* (cat. no. 26, p. 68), an anti-Nazi caricature by Dorothea Wüsten Koeppen.[32] This image represents another, quite distinct approach to mother and child relations and offers insight into the views of the Third Reich toward mothers and children. With almost cartoonlike clarity and unmistakable irony, Koeppen portrays a happy blond mother with her small daughter in tow and an unidentified child in a baby carriage decorated by a small Nazi flag. They are walking along a spotless street named Hindenburg (after the president of the Weimar Republic who appointed Hitler chancellor), in front of a bakery with a park in the background. The picture represents a satiric

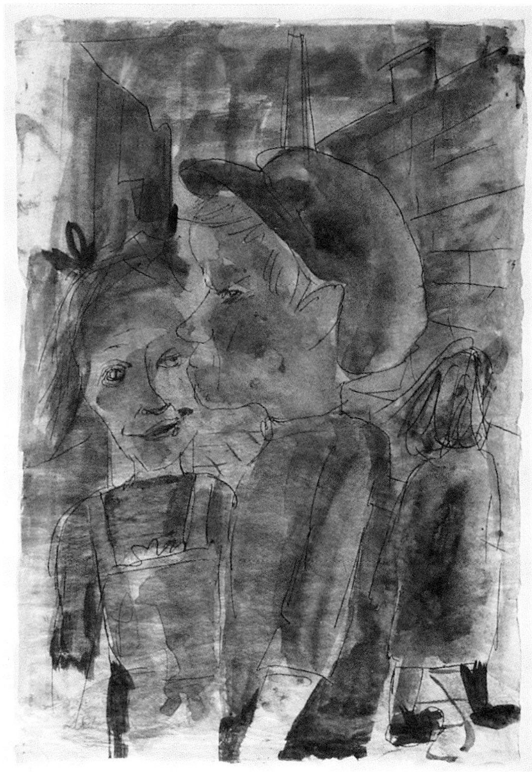

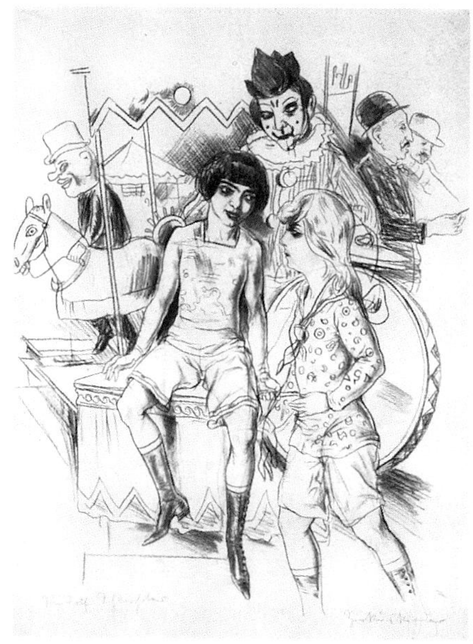

Rudolf Schlichter, *Circus Children (Zirkuskinder)*, c. 1924-25? (cat. no. 42)

Otto Dix, *Workers' Children (Arbeiterkinder)*, 1922 (cat. no. 15)

look at the ideology of the Third Reich with respect to its encouragement of women to produce the children necessary to achieve the aims of the *Volk.* Work opportunities and other rights of women were linked to the possibility of their being mothers, and the German state offered marriage incentives, including stipends and tax credits, for "certifiably Aryan" parents, particularly where the women volunteered to leave the work force and focus on childbearing. Birth control and abortions were made illegal, and a bachelor's tax was imposed on the unmarried. The value placed on children in this context is their use in fulfilling the aims of the state.

The angst and suffering undergone by poor and needy children is a major theme of *Neue Sachlichkeit* artists. For further insight into the plight of these children it is necessary to consider other pictures from the era. Dix's *Workers' Children*, 1922 (cat. no. 15) portrays an adolescent boy and girl against the background of urban streets and factories. The shabby dress and demeanor of these children are in marked contrast to that of the fashionably dressed puppetlike boy and girl in *Sunday Outing*. Poverty over affluence is evident in Dix's treatment of these proletarian children. And yet they appear more alive than their counterparts in *Sunday Outing*. The two figures in *Workers' Children* convey a sense of positive energy, and the emotional relationship between them is one of mutual attraction and possibly affection. Despite their poverty, these children might well have been the hope of the future. Dix's exquisite rendering of the scene in watercolor reinforces the life-affirming qualities of the subjects.

Other perspectives on the lives of the urban poor and those perhaps more fortunately located in rural settings are reflected in paintings such as Fritz Burmann's *Farmer's Children (Two Children with a Hare)*, 1923 (cat. no. 6, p. 68); Karl Holtz's *Farmer's Child*, c. 1921 (cat. no. 22, p. 40); Bernhard Kretzschmar's *Standing Boy*, 1921 (cat. no. 27, p. 40); Wilhelm Lachnit's *Boy in Sailor Suit*, 1923 (cat. no. 28, p. 40); and Alice Sommer's *Two Sisters*, 1925 (cat. no. 46, p. 40). Virtually all of these images exemplify the plight of children of angst and profound sadness, whether indicative of their own feelings or a broader cultural malaise. These children suffer from lack of basic material and psychological support, perhaps alienated from an adult world unable to meet their essential needs.

Not all of the pictures in this era fit the somber view of children under duress represented in the *Neue Sachlichkeit* mode. Ernst Fritsch's *Son of the Shoemaker,* 1922 (cat. no. 19, p. 72) pictures a boy wearing a striped shirt and jeans, framed by the doorway of his family's prosperous business. Martel Schwichtenberg' *Girl in Red Striped Skirt*, c. 1920 (cat. no. 43, p. 69), painted under the influence of the Expressionist Paula Modersohn-Becker, depicts a shy young farm girl (probably from the region of the Worpswede artist's colony) with loving compassion.[33] A similar feeling is expressed toward the child at play in Otto Herbig's *The Sick Boy*, 1923 (cat. no. 21, p. 69). In this picture, Herbig functions as a sensitive observer who takes the viewer into the child's world without being intrusive. This child (the artist's two-year-old son), playing in his attic room, suffers some illness as indicated by his loss of hair and the sadness on his face; yet he seems loved and protected, and far away from the problems of children who are sometimes required to live under threat from poverty and abuse. Julius Hüther's *Pleasures of Winter,* 1931 (cat. no. 23, p. 70) shows an elegantly dressed young child guiding a sled down a snowy slope, with skiers in the background. The pleasure brought by the sleigh ride, surrounded by the beauty of nature, erases all thoughts of angst and tragedy in a moment of pure joy. Yet it is possible that this image, like Dix's *Sunday Outing,* contains an ironic message. In the back of the scene the skiers appear to be crashing, perhaps a symbol of underlying societal discontent.

As with other periods of art history, there is the question of sexuality and the possible abuse of children. Of the *Neue Sachlichkeit* and related Expressionist works considered here, two works, Ernest Neuschul's *Nude Girl,* 1930 (cat. no. 35, p. 69) and Rudolf Schlichter's *Circus Children*, c. 1924-25 (cat. no. 42, p. 22) require comment with respect to this theme. *Nude Girl* shows a young girl of dark skin and hair seated on the edge of a bed facing the viewer with her body fully exposed. The small and sparse room signifies an environment of poverty. It is entirely possible that the young girl, depicted here in the beginning stages of puberty, is a child prostitute. Her downcast head and posture intimate that she is a victim of deprivation. And the environment suggests deprivation and possibly other forms of neglect and abuse. With Schlichter's *Circus Children*, the matter is much clearer. Here is an unambiguous representation with overtones of sexuality. The leering clown figure towers over two young girls. But these girls are far from innocent, as one is holding a knife, perhaps intended as a phallic symbol, pointed in the direction of her friend's abdomen.

Modernist Works

The next grouping of pictures in the exhibition consists of images by modernist painters of the twentieth century. There is no consistent theme in these works; rather, they reflect a diversity of styles and approaches to children. In some instances, the concerns are mainly aesthetic, as in Odilon Redon's *Portrait of a Young Boy*, c. 1906 (cat. no. 38, p. 25). This work is one of numerous portraits painted by Redon on commission after the turn of the century when he turned to portraiture as a part of a marketing strategy to build his artistic reputation. This child's head is beautifully rendered in lush pastels of yellow, blue, green, and black. Color was used by Redon for its suggestive powers. Here, he uses color and the delicate lines that form the profile of the sitter's head to convey a sense of the sitter's presence. The picture exemplifies the artist's view that a portrait ought to be capable of enabling the viewer to sense the sitter's presence from his face. When elaborating upon his views on portraiture, the artist stressed the importance of having a sitter for whom he felt sympathy, namely a head and a soul that pleased him. According to Redon, the portrait is "about human beauty with all the prestige thought can bring to it." He believed that "Everything that is incapable of moving us is of no value."[34] The subject in *Portrait of a Young Boy* is clearly from a privileged upbringing and is devoid of any hint of need or abuse from society.

The young adolescent pictured in Scottish painter John Quinton Pringle's *Portrait of a Boy: A Reluctant Subject*, 1910 (cat. no. 37, p. 25) is a different matter. The sitter is a boy from one of the poorest districts in Glasgow whom Pringle befriended.[35] He is specially dressed in a "Sunday suit" that he wears uncomfortably. His reluctance as a subject is revealed in his stiff posture and distrusting gaze. The subject is positioned near a garden wall and surrounded by flowers in a decidedly non-masculine setting. What are we to make of such a picture? Does it record a contrast of social class and values between the subject and the artist? The subject seems beyond the age of innocence, and yet the picture appears invasive, if not exploitative. The picture is painted in a Post-Impressionist manner where color and form draw attention to the decorative aspect of its surface. The effect of the painter's technique thus tends to distance the viewer from its subject matter.

John Quinton Pringle
Portrait of a Boy: A Reluctant Subject, 1910
(cat. no. 37)

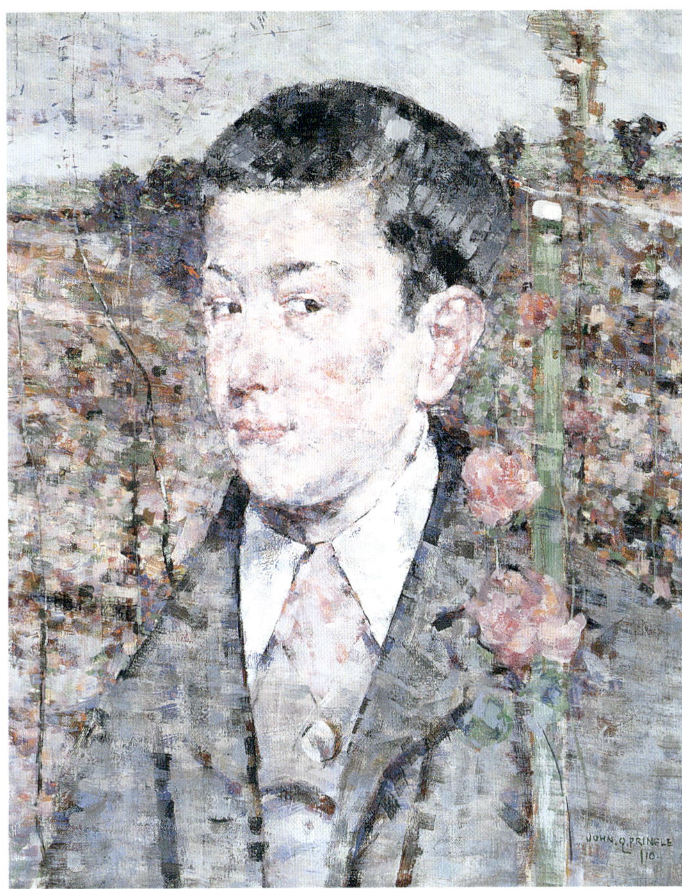

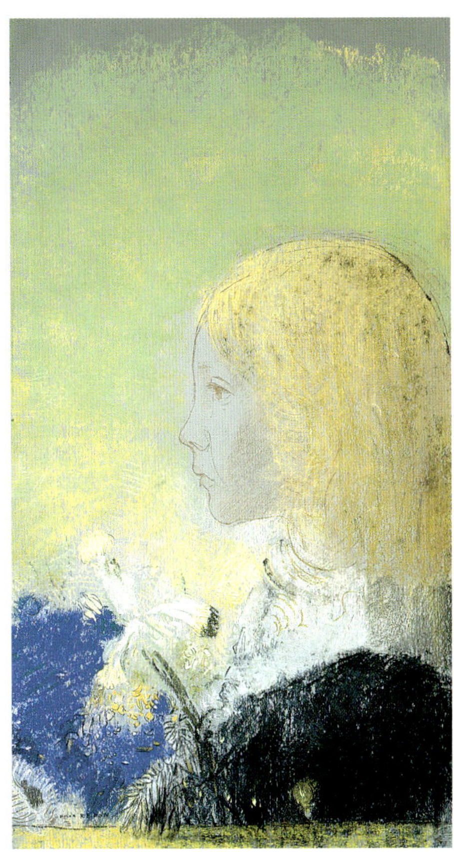

Odilon Redon
Portrait of a Young Boy
(Portrait d'un jeune garçon), c. 1906
(cat. no. 38)

Gabriele Münter, like Redon, believed that portraits demanded that the artist produce a symbol of the spiritual aura of the person being depicted. "Art was another means for her to approach the spiritual in an individual, especially as the portrait interpreted physiognomy subjectively to make visible the invisible core of the person depicted."[36] Her approach to the subject of children appears to be generic and primarily aesthetic, as was Redon's. She is concerned with formalist issues relating to the language of painting rather than with the social or maternal aspects of the subject. *Girl with Doll,* 1908-09 (cat. no. 34, p. 71) portrays a young girl with bare feet, in a red dress, seated and holding in her lap a doll dressed in light blue.[37] Simplification of the compositional features of color, figuration, and pictorial space in this picture reflects the influence of Bavarian folk art and the reverse-glass painting of Murnau, which features contours "with heavy black outlines, broad flat color areas and the absence of shading three-dimensionality."[38] The free spatial orientation of the painting may also have been influenced by Münter's interest in children's art. *Girl with Doll* was painted in the same year that Münter began collecting children's art. Münter, together with Kandinsky, collected the art of children and drew upon it as a source for a new vocabulary in their respective art styles. The imaginative power, expressive authenticity, and indifference to practical meaning found in children's art appealed to Münter and to *Der Blaue Reiter* group painting in Munich at the beginning of the twentieth century. They saw in this art the possibility of subverting the influences of culture and individual perspective in search of a universal language of art.[39]

Joaquín Sorolla y Bastida was a nineteenth-century Spanish realist from Valencia with an Impressionist palette and a passion for light. He banished the earth tones and dark shadows of the Spanish masters. His ability to capture the movement, color, and radiant light surrounding a figure on the sun-flooded beach of his native land is exemplified in the painting *Drawing in the Sand*, c. 1911 (cat. no. 47, p. 70). The subject is a nude boy at the seaside kneeling with arm extended while drawing in the sand what appears to be a sailboat. The child is happily engaged in the action, and the mood is warm and friendly. The artist provides a spontaneous rendering of the scene, capturing the natural rhythmic flow of the boy's movements with his fluid brushstrokes. The representation of childhood provided here is one of living in paradise, in a state of happiness and innocence. This image shows the child enjoying beautiful nature, loved and well cared for, and without any hint of discord or impoverishment.

Chaim Soutine painted many children and is represented in this exhibition by *Children and Geese*, 1934 (cat. no. 48, p. 71). The image is of two children walking hand-in-hand down a country road, passing by some geese; the child on the left is painted in blue, the one on the right in red. Behind the two children is a landscape densely painted in verdant and earth tones. Both the figures and the landscape are full of pathos and energy, heightened by thick impasto applied in the artist's Expressionist style. The expression on the children's faces reflects isolation and loneliness, even sadness, possibly a projection of the artist's feelings from his own unsettled childhood. The mood of Soutine's children contrasts sharply with the happy expression of the child in Sorolla y Bastida's *Drawing in the Sand*. Despite the pastoral setting, the children in Soutine's painting convey a sense of anxiety that is reinforced by the energy of the artist's expressive pictorial surface.

American Social Realists

The final group of pictures in the exhibition consists of paintings by three American social realists: Philip Evergood, Raphael Soyer, and Jacob Lawrence. Evergood's *Laughing Boy*, 1945 (cat. no. 16, p. 72), is the work of a well-tutored artist who often uses art as a means of political commentary. Evergood's complex style incorporates Realist and Expressionist elements, laced with a touch of the fantastic and the bizarre. In this picture, the artist depicts a young boy from the waist up, holding a huge slice of watermelon in his hands. Endowed with dark hair, dark eyes, and medium-toned skin, the boy is dressed in a red-and white-striped polo shirt. His face and the watermelon dominate the foreground, while the background is filled with sky and a cluster of trees. On the surface, Evergood's picture gives the appearance of a happy, innocent child about to sample the pleasures of the tasty watermelon. On another level, however, this picture can be seen as a satirical commentary on racial stereotypes where watermelon is a common staple in images of blacks from the rural south.

At age thirteen, Raphael Soyer fled Tsarist Russia with his family when they were banished for their association with young revolutionaries. His humanistic approach to art is the product of his experiences in a proletarian lower-middle-class Jewish family in New York. As a figurative realist, his approach to art is American rather than European in tone, as the *Portrait of a Young Girl*, c. 1946 (cat. no. 49, p. 81) shows. Its appealing qualities are directness, clarity, and simplicity, largely unaffected by the sophistication of Surrealism, Abstract Expressionism, or other developments in modern art. The subject is a girl of approximately fourteen years of age wearing a red top and rolled-up jeans, with a small black spaniel. The girl is barefoot, with her dark hair in long braids. Her face is somber, perhaps because she is contemplating the uncertainties of a changing world, or possibly only the changes brought on by her personal metamorphosis from childhood to adulthood. In any event, the picture is an icon of early teen years during the 1940s, charming, hopeful, yet harboring uncertainties in a post-war era.

Our last image is Jacob Lawrence's *Birth*, 1948 (cat. no. 29, p. 28). Lawrence took art classes in the New Deal WPA arts project of the 1930s and was influenced by the 1930s environment of social conscience. He works in a style informed by narrative content and often featuring serial imagery. His subjects are the concerns of African-American history and culture, and his themes are drawn from "everyday life in the black community and the historic struggles of oppressed peoples."[40] The image of childhood represented in *Birth* removes any thought that the idealized images found in the age of Romantic innocence or in Renoir's mother-and-child pictures represent a universal state of being. Lawrence is closer in spirit to the *Neue Sachlichkeit* artists. In the foreground of this enigmatic image is a mother, perhaps a prostitute, standing on the street in the cold, wearing a fur coat. Behind her, in the distance, is her newborn child, perhaps already abandoned in its infancy, or partially so by the necessities of the mother's attending to issues of economic survival.

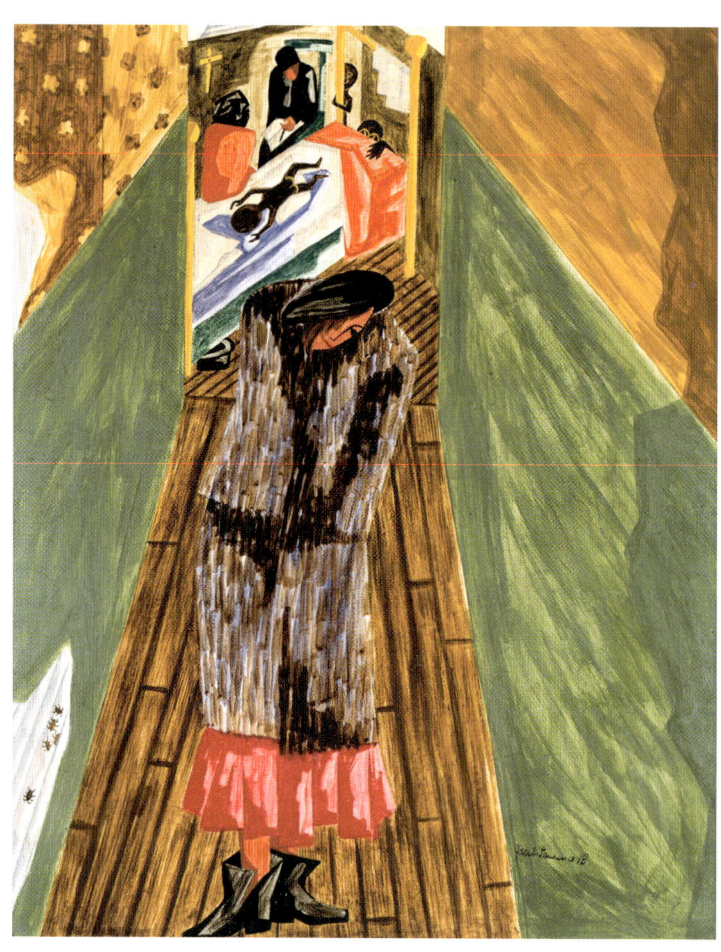

Jacob Lawrence
Birth, 1948
(cat. no. 29)

After 1950

Artists' representations of children have continued to evolve as society's views of children and the world of childhood have changed. The exhibition documents some of these changes as they appear in works created before 1950. An increasingly complex society now requires continuous rethinking of how artists portray children. As the practice of featuring children in art extends beyond the closing date of the exhibition, we see that the representation of children is always a matter of the prevailing artistic conventions. For some artists today, photography has become the medium of choice, but others continue to paint. Examples of more recent works in the paintings of Timothy Cummings and James Rosenquist indicate that figurative art and social commentary continue to have an important role. Timothy Cummings' *Children with Dead Bird*, 1997, is a disturbing surreal image of a young boy and girl. The girl is wearing a white ruffled dress with three large roses in her hair. She clutches a dead bird in her hand, and there are blood smears on her face and dress. The boy is naked except for a blue and white ribbon with bows laid across his upper body. He also has blood smears on his

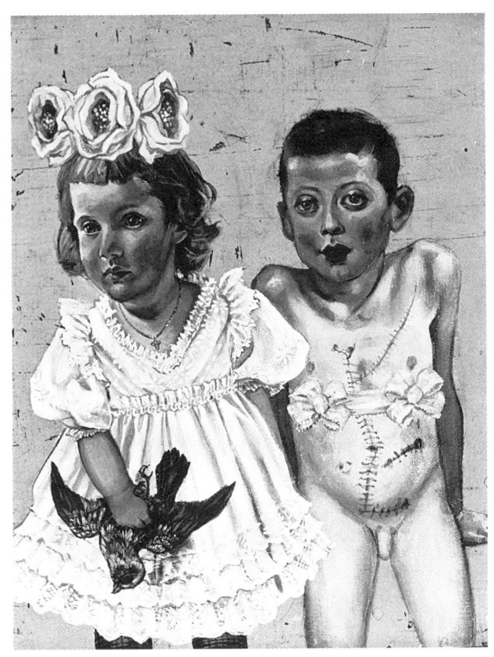

Timothy Cummings, *Children with Dead Bird,* 1997

cheeks, and is marked with multiple rows of surgical stitching from wounds across his chest and abdomen. Both children appear to be victims. James Rosenquist's enigmatic *Growth Plan,* 1966 (p. 30) is equally disturbing. His painting features nine boys of varying ages and heights arranged horizontally across a grid formed by the lines of a playing field. The boys all wear swimming trunks and shoes, while they stand at attention with arms at their sides in quasi-military fashion. What is the painting's message? Are these children being assembled to fit into predetermined roles in a world devoid of imagination or humanity? The message of regimentation and conformity found in *Growth Plan* is as disturbing as the abuse in Cummings' work. These are but a sample of the work that continues with respect to children in art.

Since 1950, there have been numerous changes in attitudes toward children and in artwork representing children. Adults have become more deeply involved in the adult-child relationship. In many instances this relationship is a natural and mutually nurturing experience. However, there is a growing concern when children become objects of adult gratification and desire which crosses the boundaries into exploitation. Also, gender roles have become more fluid as fathers share nurturing duties with working mothers.

Outside the family, the shift from agrarian to industrial societies, and now to a society based on communications technology, has brought about significant changes in the way childhood is viewed. Throughout all of these changes, children have continued to participate in the labor force in varying degrees. But their participation is limited, and children are protected in this sphere by mandatory school requirements and child labor laws. On the other hand, increased career demands on working parents in the second half of the twentieth century often conflict with child care responsibilities. With these changes come shifts with respect to roles for children. Expectations are high for children to perform in school, to compete in athletics, and perhaps also to occupy part-time jobs. Peer group relations are often more important than family and frequently extend to anti-social behaviors such as gang activities. Inexplicable acts of violence by children occur with alarming frequency. Increasingly, children are targets of marketing for items ranging from consumer products to drugs. The Internet has substantially elevated the access of children to information of

James Rosenquist,
Growth Plan, 1966

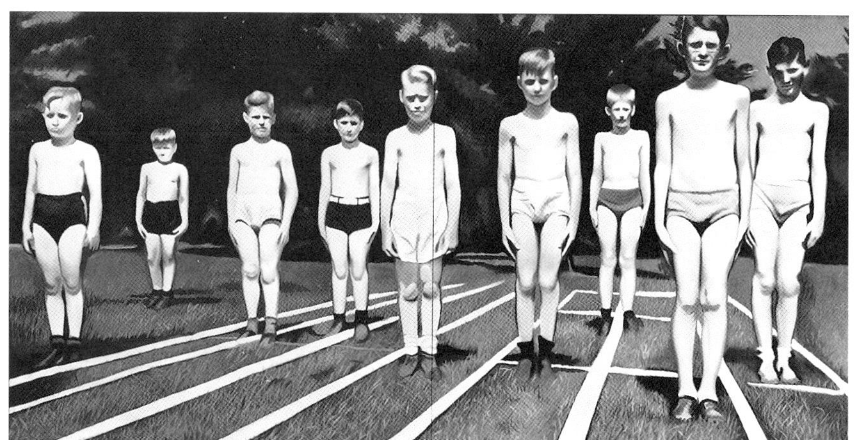

all sorts ranging from art and science to pornography. The boundaries between adulthood and childhood continue to recede as children acquire a knowledge of technology that exceeds their parents' knowledge. It is within the context provided by these circumstances that artists will continue to explore the concept of children in art.

Notes

1. Cotton Mather, *Diary of Cotton Mather* (1681-1708) (Boston: Massachusetts Historical Society, 1911), vol. 7, p. 536. Cited in Sandra Brandt and Elissa Cullman, *Small Folk: A Celebration of Childhood in America* (New York: E.P. Dutton in association with the Museum of American Folk Art, 1980), p. 125.
2. John Locke, *Some Thoughts Concerning Education* (London, 1693).
3. Jean-Jacques Rousseau, *Émile*, 1762.
4. Robert Rosenblum, *The Romantic Child: From Runge to Sendak* (London: Thames and Hudson, 1988).
5. Carol Duncan, "Happy Mothers and Other New Ideas in French Art," *Art Bulletin* LV (December 1973), pp. 570-83.
6. Anne Higonnet, *Pictures of Innocence: The History and Crisis of Ideal Childhood* (London: Thames and Hudson, 1998).
7. The nineteenth-century photographer Julia Margaret Cameron also explored the identity of women and children in her work. See Sylvia Wolf, *Julia Margaret Cameron's Women* (Chicago and New Haven, Conn.: The Art Institute of Chicago and Yale University Press, 1998).
8. Higonnet, *Pictures of Innocence*, pp. 24, 28.
9. See Hugh Cunningham, *The Children of the Poor: Representations of Childhood Since the Seventeenth Century* (Oxford and Cambridge, Mass.: Basil Blackwell, Inc., 1991), and *Hard Times: Social Realism in Victorian Art*, Julian Treuherz, ed. (London: Lund Humphries Publishers Ltd in association with Manchester City Art Galleries, 1987).
10. Anita Schorsch, *Images of Childhood: An Illustrated Social History* (New York: Mayflower Books, Inc., 1979), pp. 136-149. Also, *Images of the Child*, Harry Eiss, ed. (Bowling Green, Ohio, 1994), pp. 10-11.
11. Schorsch, *Images of Childhood*, p. 142.
12. Schorsch, *Images of Childhood*, p. 137.
13. Simone de Beauvoir, *The Second Sex*, trans. H. M. Parshley (New York: Alfred A. Knopf, Inc. 1953; reprint, 1993), pp. 281-425. See also James R. Kincaid, *Child-Loving: The Erotic Child and Victorian Culture* (New York and London: Routledge, 1992), pp. 172-75.
14. Higonnet, *Pictures of Innocence*, pp. 201-5.
15. The nineties have seen a new scholarly interest in the meaning of children in culture. See Scott Heller, "The Meaning of Children in Culture Becomes a Focal Point for Scholars," *The Chronicle of Higher Education*, 7 August 1998, for a review of recent books. Among the titles noted are: Paula S. Fass, *Kidnapped: Child Abduction in America*,

1998; James R. Kincaid, *Child-Loving: The Erotic Child and Victorian Culture,* 1992; Nancy Scheper-Hughes and Carolyn Sargent, eds., *Small Wars: The Cultural Politics of Childhood,* 1998; Philip Jenkins, *Moral Panic: Changing Concepts of the Child Molestor in Modern America;* James Marten, *The Children's Civil War,* 1998; and Higonnet, *Pictures of Innocence,* 1998.

16. Frère established at Ecóven near Paris a colony of child painters that on occasion included Mary Cassatt.
17. Schorsch, *Images of Childhood,* p. 98.
18. "Jozef Israels," *Selected Works* (Milwaukee: Patrick and Beatrice Haggerty Museum of Art, Marquette University, 1984), pp. 62-63.
19. Cassatt was a dedicated printmaker who produced more than two hundred prints over thirty years. *Peasant Mother and Child* was exhibited in her first major exhibition in the United States held at the Durand-Ruel Gallery in New York in 1895.
20. Anne Higonnet, *Berthe Morisot's Images of Women* (Cambridge, Mass.: Harvard University Press, 1992), p. 218.
21. Judith A. Barter, "Mary Cassatt: Themes, Sources, and the Modern Woman: Childhood and Maternity," in *Mary Cassatt: Modern Woman,* exh. cat. (Chicago: The Art Institute of Chicago in association with Harry N. Abrams, 1998), p. 76.
22. Christopher Riopelle, "Pierre-Auguste Renoir: Mother and Child," in *Great French Paintings from the Barnes Foundation* (New York: Alfred A. Knopf in association with Lincoln University Press, 1993), pp. 56-58. Renoir was inspired by Raphael's mother and child pictures which he observed during a visit to Italy in 1881. The picture is intended to reflect the spontaneous innocence of a young Italian girl with a child. On the other hand, see Renoir's *Madame Renoir with Pierre,* 1886, in which Aline is seen nursing Renoir's oldest son, Pierre. The picture, which shows the child nursing at the mother's exposed breast, is as sensuous and intimate as any of Cassatt's mother and child images. Reproduced in *Paintings by Renoir* (Chicago: The Art Institute of Chicago, 1973), no. 52.
23. Robert Hobbs, *Milton Avery* (New York: Hudson Hills Press, 1990), p. 54.
24. Daniel Robbins, ed., *Jacques Villon* (Cambridge, Mass.: Fogg Art Museum, Harvard University, 1976), p. 168. See also *Jacques Villon,* exh. cat. (Oslo: Kunstnernes Hus, 1960), cat. no. 44 for a reference to Villon's *Grande Maternité.*
25. Fronia E. Wissman, *Bouguereau* (San Francisco: Pomegranate ArtBooks, 1996), pp. 59-62.
26. Joseph Kosuth, *The Play of the Unmentionable* (New York: The New Press in association with the Brooklyn Museum, 1992).
27. Higonnet, *Berthe Morisot's Images of Women,* p. 230.
28. Higonnet, *Berthe Morisot's Images of Women,* pp. 233-34.
29. See *Paintings by Renoir.*
30. A variation of this painting, *Enfant aux fleurs,* 1915, from the collection of Catherine and David A. Straz, Jr., shows the child with flowers instead of ribbons. For other examples of Vuillard's paintings of children see Andrew Carnduff Ritchie, *Edouard Vuillard* (New York: The Museum of Modern Art, 1954): *Reading,* 1893, p. 42; *Mother and Child,* c. 1900, p. 55; *Child in a Room,* c. 1900, p. 74; *Annette's Lunch,* 1901, p. 75; *The Painter Ker-Xavier Roussel and his Daughter,* c. 1902, p. 76; and *Girl with a Doll,* 1906, p. 83.
31. Reinhold Heller, *Art in Germany 1909-1936: From Expressionism to Resistance: The Marvin and Janet Fishman Collection,* exh. cat. (Munich: Prestel in association with the Milwaukee Art Museum, 1990), p. 172.
32. Information concerning this picture is taken from Heller, *Art in Germany,* p. 194.
33. Heller, *Art in Germany,* p. 223.
34. Maryanne Stevens, "Redon's Artistic and Critical Position," in *Odilon Redon: Prince of Dreams 1840-1916,* exh. cat. (Chicago: The Art Institute of Chicago, 1994), p. 294.
35. Information provided by Artemis Fine Arts, Inc., London and New York.
36. Reinhold Heller, *Gabriel Münter: The Years of Expressionism 1903-1920,* exh. cat. (Munich and New York: Prestel, 1997), p. 111.
37. Heller, *Gabriel Münter,* cat. no. 28, pp. 113, 118.
38. Heller, *Gabriel Münter,* p. 115.
39. Jonathan Fineberg, "In Search of Universality: The Vasily Kandinsky and Gabriele Münter Collection," in *The Innocent Eye: Children's Art and the Modern Artist* (Princeton, N. J.: Princeton University Press, 1997), pp. 46-81.
40. Patricia Hills, "Jacob Lawrence," in *National Museum of American Art* (Washington, D. C.: Smithsonian Institution, 1995), p. 95.

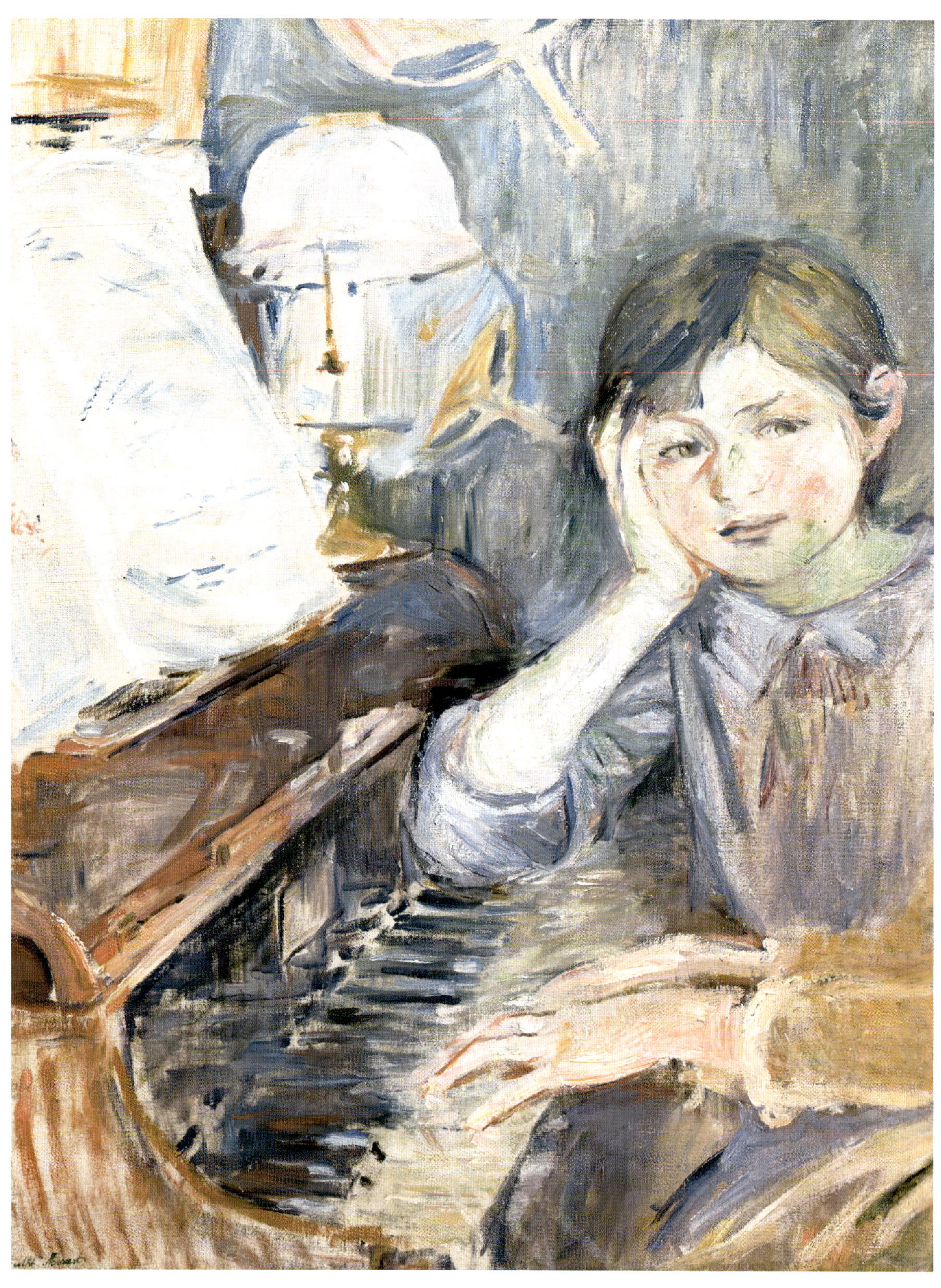

Berthe Morisot, *Julie Listening (Julie écoutant)*, 1888 (cat. no. 33)

Pictures We Like to Look At

ANNE HIGONNET

Children make cute pictures. Or do they? Cute pictures make bad paintings. Or do they? The intersection between two histories produced the paintings in this exhibition: the history of childhood, and the history of modernist painting. One is a history of ideas, the other is a history of esthetics. These two histories are not at all identical, and their differences go a long way toward explaining the differences among the paintings in this exhibition. One history made ideal children look cute. The other made cute paintings look bad.

Children in pictures made before about 1700 were not just cute. Although they may have been intended secondarily to appeal in an easy way to lighter sentiments, they were primarily intended to represent the great passions of adult life—the most profound theological arguments, the most lustful desires, and the most material social ambitions. "Cute" denotes innocence, and the children in pre-modern pictures were not entirely innocent. If children in art were supposed to be human, they represented future adult social status. With few exceptions (Breughel, Murillo, Rembrandt, sometimes Van Dyck), the children who appear in paintings were the offspring of royal or aristocratic families, and the point of their portraits was to make their lineage manifest. They are placed within family homes and in front of family land, the seats of their power and signs of their rank. They wear small versions of adult clothing and are posed according to adult conventions. Linked to their parents, either explicitly within group family portraits, or implicitly, the children in pre-modern art promise dynastic continuity and display wealth. Even in seventeenth-century Dutch art, the prototype of modern middle-class art, children tend to illustrate maxims and proverbs of adult life.

If the children were not supposed to be human, they represented divine knowledge. Pagan cupids embodied Eros, the force of lust, while Christian cherubs accompanied biblical figures, celebrating, lamenting, and demonstrating moral lessons. As to the Christ Child, shown with his Madonna mother, He is Himself an omniscient God, one who takes human form but remains divine. In his book *The Sexuality of Christ in Renaissance Art and in Modern Oblivion,* Leo Steinberg has convincingly argued that the display of the holy child's flesh serves a crucial theological function by rendering visible the incarnation of God.[1] Moreover, the symbols of crucifixion included in Madonna and Child paintings remind us that both mother and son know the terrible future in store for them. Already offered to us in a way by the painting, as the object of our gaze, the Christ Child solemnly accepts his fate, as does his sorrowful mother.

By the end of the eighteenth century, notions of childhood had radically changed. Historians disagree about the exact timing of this change, but all agree it did happen. Philippe Ariès, in his pioneering *Centuries of Childhood,* argued that adults cared rather little even for their own children before the seventeenth century, and that the idea of childhood as a distinct age to be treasured and protected emerged only in modern times.[2] Other historians have since disagreed with Ariès, arguing for a much earlier and more intense appreciation of childhood. In any case, by the eighteenth-century Enlightenment, several concepts essential to a new attitude were widely accepted among affluent Europeans: a private, nurturing middle-class nuclear family as the building block of society, a capitalist opposition between masculine public and feminine domestic spheres, and a political belief in the innate worth of the individual.

Together, these concepts fostered a sheltered, mothering domain within which childhood could exist apart. Frederick Waugh's 1887 *The Artist's Family at Home* (cat. no. 57, p. 61) epitomizes this modern domain of Romantic childhood. Both the title of the picture and its iconography identify the subject as a middle-class mother caring for her own baby and daughter. Discretely yet fashionably affluent clothing and decorative art objects reinforce the painting's message. The scene is entirely withdrawn from the outside, adult, working world. It is also an exemplary scene; the daughter's emulation of her mother's maternal behavior cues us to model ourselves on this ideal image. Even when childhood is ostensibly set elsewhere than the maternal home, as in Norbert Goeneutte's 1889 *Reine Goeneutte Washing the Young Jean Geurard in the Artist's Studio* (cat. no. 20, p. 61), the interior intimacy of the relationship between innocently naked child and caring middle-class mother reproduces the pattern. By the end of the nineteenth century, the Romantic ideal had become so deeply ingrained in the modern, middle-class, western imagination that it could be projected onto any time, class, or place. Jozef Israëls's c.1898 *Dutch*

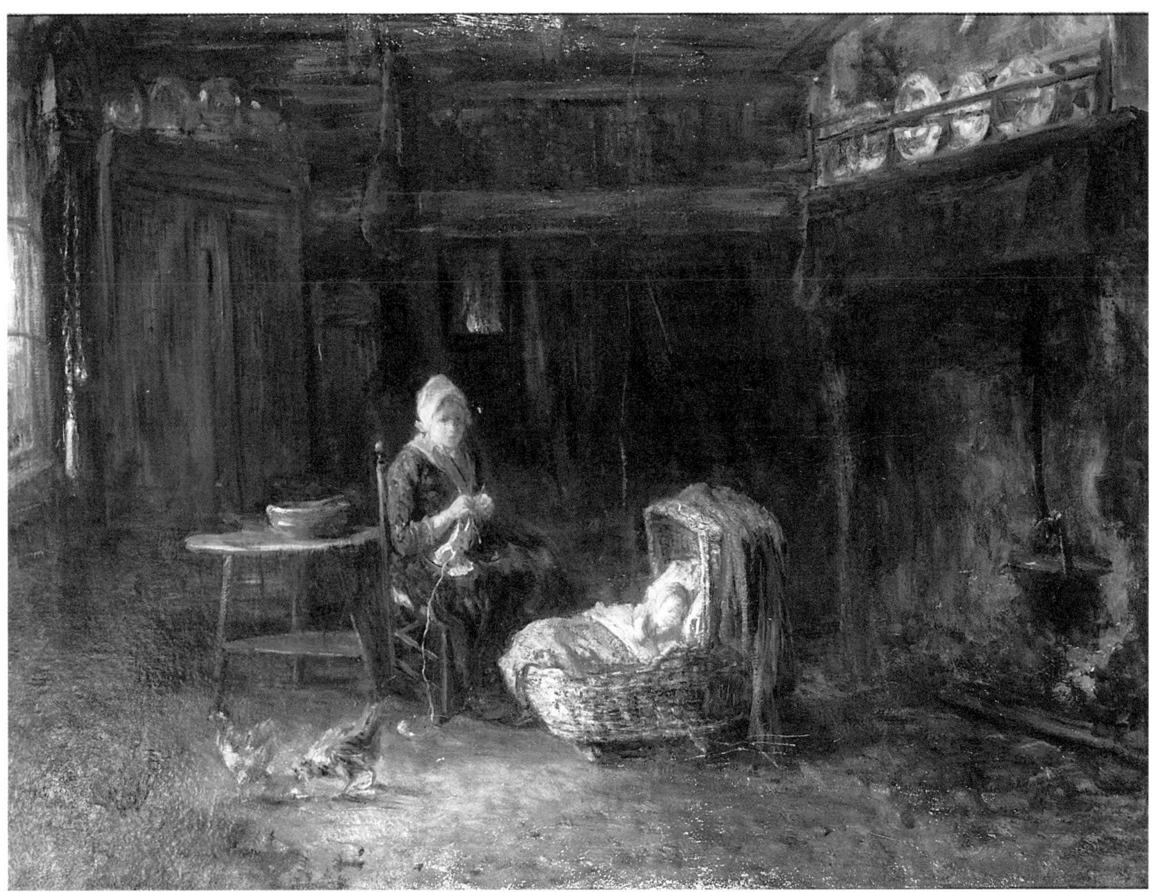

Jozef Israëls, *Dutch Interior* (called *Mother and Child*), c. 1898 (cat. no. 24)

Interior (cat. no. 24), significantly also called *Mother and Child,* makes the Romantic ideal look timeless and classless by casting a maternal scene in a traditional peasant setting. Whatever the difficult realities of rearing children might have been for peasants, they were not suitable material for Israëls's contemporary urban audience.

It had taken a long time for pictures like *The Artist's Family at Home* and *Mother and Child* to look so natural and normal. Their assumptions about childhood could be taken so much for granted because they were the outcome of more than a century's brilliant pictorial invention, dating back to the great eighteenth-century British portraitists. The first consistent and influential visualizations of modern Romantic childhood were the work of painters like Sir Joshua Reynolds, Thomas Lawrence, Thomas Gainsborough, Sir Henry Raeburn, and John Hoppner. In their paintings, children were imagined to be absorbed in a world of their own, a world identified with nature. Unconscious of adults and the adult world, these new Romantic children gamboled in edenic scenery and played with toys, pets, or each other. Physically, the Romantic child was also differentiated from adults, not only by wearing clothing designed only for children, but also by being pictured asexually. The sight of a child's body was transformed into a vision of innocence. Where previous art had insisted on the divisions of rank, British portraits instead insisted on differentiation by age.

The level at which the invention of modern childhood took place was high. Though eighteenth-century British art was being in some ways transformed by industrialization and urbanization, the audience for which painters like Reynolds and Lawrence worked was intellectually, financially, and socially elite. The childhood they represented was correspondingly particular. Romantic ideas of childhood innocence and fragility did not apply to any children who were not affluent and European. Harsh labor conditions for working-class or colonized children, as well as the exploitation of their sexuality, remained widely accepted for several decades. But as the western middle class expanded during the early decades of the nineteenth century, the concept of Romantic childhood spread, and so did a demand for pictures of that concept. The same class that created a pervasive Victorian culture of the child could now afford pictures. But what kind of pictures? As the middle class expanded, it fragmented. While the upper reaches of the middle class might be educated and wealthy enough to want paintings of the sort the great portraitists of the previous century had created, the middle-middle-class and lower-middle-class echelons were not. As the audience for pictures splintered, so did picture making. For several centuries, a type of painting called genre had flourished in a marginal way. Scenes of everyday life, genre painting ranked low in the strict Academic hierarchy of painting subjects and therefore did not tend to attract the most gifted and ambitious artists or patrons. Nonetheless, genre painting could be considered a minor aspect of a basically homogeneous field. In the early decades of the nineteenth century, by contrast, no one kind of artistic authority was able to maintain one hegemonic hierarchy of value. While Academies remained powerful, the expanding middle-class market for art made genre painting a newly lucrative and prestigious endeavor. Moreover, genre painting became more aligned along middle-class interests than it ever had before, reinforcing in ways both blatant and subtle middle-class beliefs about self, genius, gender, race, and history. Pierre Édouard Frère made an entire career out of confirming a middle-class urban world view by projecting it reassuringly onto a putatively eternal peasantry. In his 1865 *Playing Mother* (cat. no. 18, p. 59), for instance, a child clad in peasant blouse and cap sits in an armchair whose eighteenth-century Louis XV style turns the painting partly into an in-joke for sophisticated furniture connoisseurs. John George Brown's c. 1880s *The Card Trick* (cat. no. 5, p. 60) also jokes, and, again, for the benefit of its designated audience. Among the boys in the painting, it

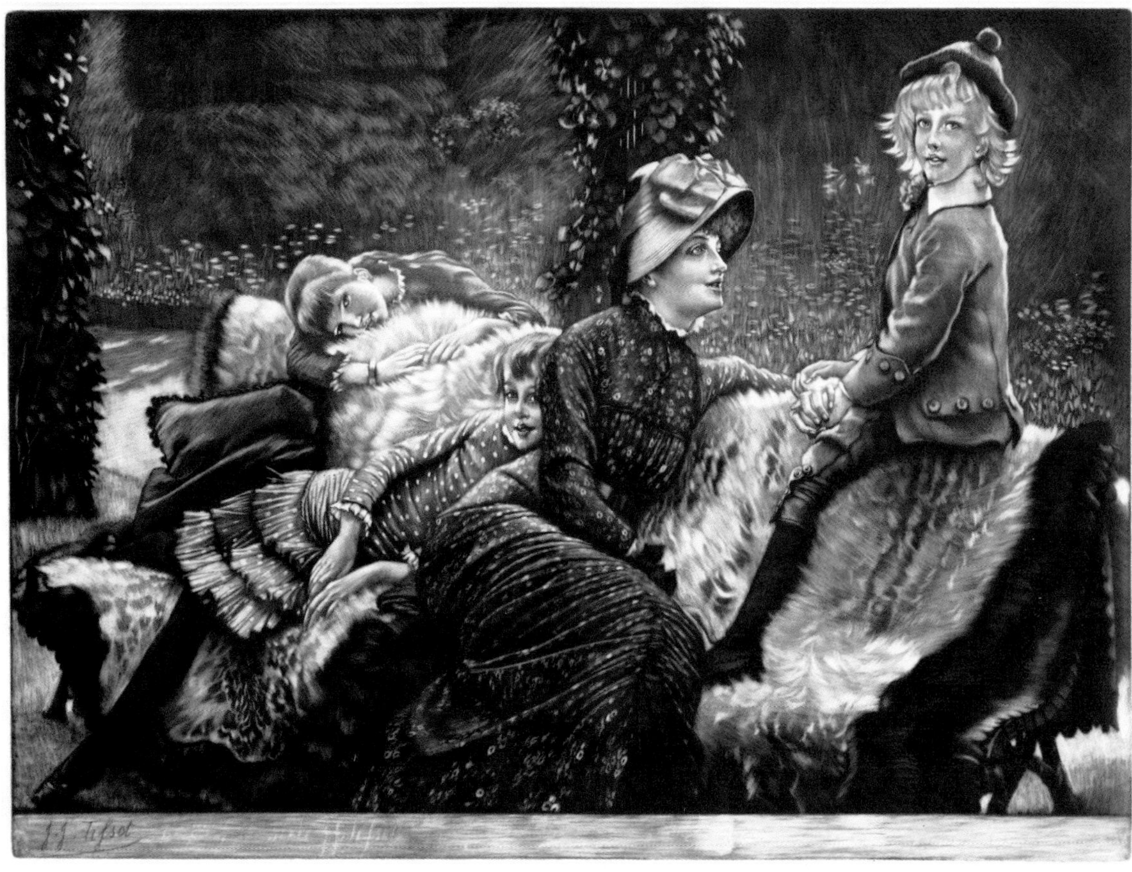

James (Jacques-Joseph) Tissot, *The Garden Bench (Le banc de jardin)*, 1883 (cat. no. 52)

is the black boy who plays the trick while the white boys enjoy themselves, stereotypically imputing the least respectable behavior in the picture to the outsider. Ernest Neuschul's 1930 *Nude Girl* (cat. no. 35, p. 69) turns its young black subject into a passive and exposed object in a way few white children would have been. Most powerfully, Jacob Lawrence's 1948 *Birth* (cat. no. 29, p. 28) radically departs from the usual scenes of happy maternity, scenes like Waugh's, when it comes to the birth of a black baby. The infant lies alone and exposed in the background, while a cloaked woman enigmatically walks away from the baby toward us, visually compressed and isolated by planes on either side of her.

By the second half of the nineteenth century, the most financially and institutionally successful painters, some of them leaders of national Academies, were primarily genre painters, in fact if not in name. Such was the case of Sir John Everett Millais in England, as well as Jean-Leon Gérôme and William Adolphe Bouguereau. Such also were the slightly later and less Academic cases of James Tissot and Joaquín Sorolla y Bastida, both of whom are represented by works in this exhibition. It is no coincidence that these painters made many pictures of children, for child-genre was one of the most successful branches of genre painting. A nineteenth-century genre picture of childhood is one that portrays an individual child without being a commissioned or individualistic portrait, or is a scene of everyday child life, a scene which may convey some moral, but which ostensibly is about the ordinary. On the whole, these genre scenes fell into five subject categories: children dressed up in special costumes, like the unusual school uniforms in Eyre Crowe's 1877 *Boys of Blue Coat School* (cat. no. 11, p. 60), especially costumes of the past—Walter Dendy Sadler's c. 1900 *The Dame's School* (cat. no. 41, p. 43), for example, with its boys wearing the wide collars, short jackets buttoned to cropped pants, and slippers worn during the earliest decades of the century and admired with nostalgia in the last decades; children with pets, like Alfred De Dreux's *Innocence between Two Thieves* (c. 1859; cat. no. 12, p. 57), which shows a girl endearingly miniaturized by two enormous dogs on either side of her, situating the child in the animal domain of nature; angels, cupids, and angel-cupid hybrids; mothers and babies, such as Waugh's *The Artist's Family at Home;* and pictures of children unconsciously prefiguring adult gender roles, like Waugh's picture, and also Frère's symptomatically titled *Playing Mother*, in which a tiny girl tenderly kisses her swaddled doll.

Genre paintings of children were tremendously popular. Even someone as exceptionally wealthy as Henry Clay Frick, who could and later did buy masterpiece paintings from many centuries and on many subjects, began by buying several nineteenth-century genre paintings of children, pictures which according to his biographer and great-granddaughter he was especially fond of.[3] Frick's child genre paintings closely resemble ones in this exhibition; particularly dear to Frick was a Bouguereau rather like *Child at Bath* (1886; cat. no. 3, p. 65), also by Bouguereau (Frick's shows a somewhat more fully dressed girl). Moreover, Frick was also typical for his time in his appreciation of prints after child genre paintings, prints which exponentially increased the visibility and hence the influence of unique paintings. Frick, for instance, owned commemorative prints of his own Bouguereau, one of which, elaborately framed, was hung in his children's playroom. The prints of children in this exhibition could have been displayed in similar ways to shape children's vision of themselves.

In their subjects and in their style, genre paintings of children closely resembled the even more popular pictures of children designed from the start to be mechanically reproduced prints. By the last quarter of the nineteenth century, illustrations by leaders in their field like Kate Greenaway had become the most widely seen pictures of children.
 Even Millais, president of the English Royal Academy, was better known around the world

for the advertisements made from his paintings of children than for anything else, including his paintings of children. In the next generation, around the turn of the century, American magazine and advertisement illustrators made the Romantic image of the child even more popular, reaching millions of viewers. Most of those viewers were women, and so were the illustrators who responded to their interests, women like Jessie Willcox Smith and Bessie Pease Gutmann. In every field of art, women were encouraged if not obliged to specialize in the subject of the child, considered suitable to their gender. Genre paintings of children were ineluctably tied to illustration's commercialization and feminization. Most importantly, genre paintings of children were tainted with the sentimentality that commercialization and feminization implied.

Because genre paintings of children are so closely associated with commerce, femininity, and above all sentimentality, they have suffered a sharp decline in critical esteem since the nineteenth century, though not always in popularity. (Some of Bouguereau's and Tissot's paintings, for instance, are more widely reproduced than ever.) Sentimentality became an accusation, not a description. The same splintering of art markets and audiences that produced nineteenth-century genre paintings of children also produced Modernism, sentimentality's implacable opponent. Modernism replaced previous barriers of birth, wealth, and education with a difficult philosophical commitment to abstraction and formalism. From its inception—in theory if not in practice—Modernism pitted itself against commercial motivations, pronounced itself masculine, and rejected sentimentality as the condition of its honesty. It was inevitable therefore that Modernism would be skeptical of the entire subject of the child.

Sentimentality was acquiring a bad intellectual reputation by the twentieth century. It is necessary to confront just how bad that reputation got to understand why some pictures in this exhibition seem bent on subverting exactly the same image of childhood that other pictures seem bent on idealizing. Confronting sentimentality and resistance to sentimentality also helps us understand why the pictures in this exhibition call for different sorts of viewing. The cultural legitimacy of sentimentality reached its nadir in the 1970s, notably because of Ann Douglas's classic 1977 *The Feminization of American Culture*. As Douglas's title immediately announces, sentimentality had become thoroughly gendered and was then considered to have been a kind of corrosive force gradually degrading nineteenth-century culture. Sentimentality had become an attribute of femininity, and of commercial culture, or should I say anti-culture, a totally pejorative attribute. Here for example is Douglas on sentiment: "sentimentalism might be defined as the political sense obfuscated or gone rancid? A relatively recent phenomenon whose appearance is linked with capitalist development, sentimentalism seeks and offers the distraction of sheer

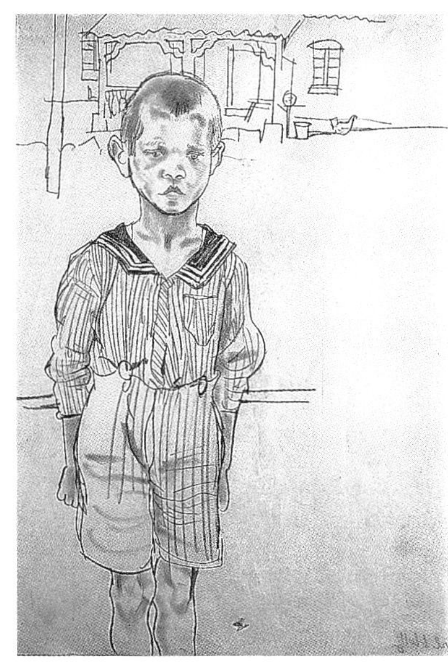

Karl Holtz
Farmer's Child
(Bauernjunge), c. 1921
(cat. no. 22)

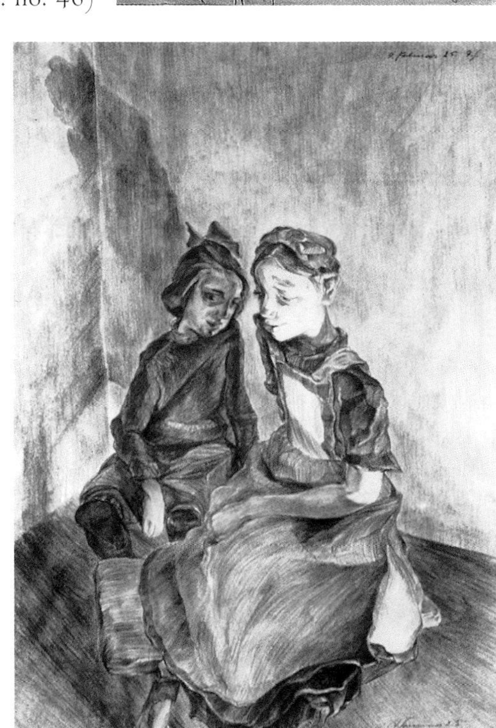

Alice Sommer
Two Sisters
(Zwei Schwestern), 1925
(cat. no. 46)

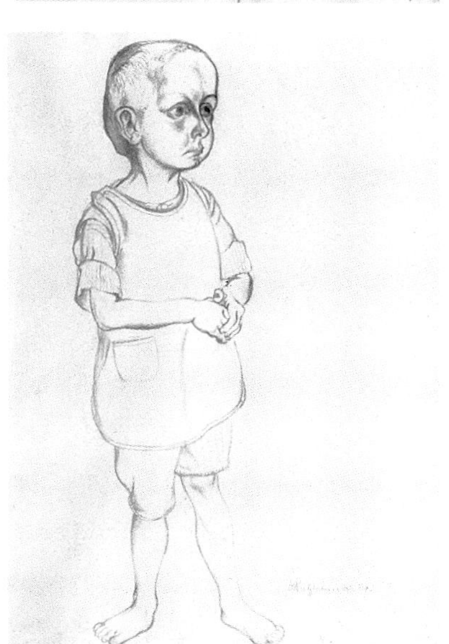

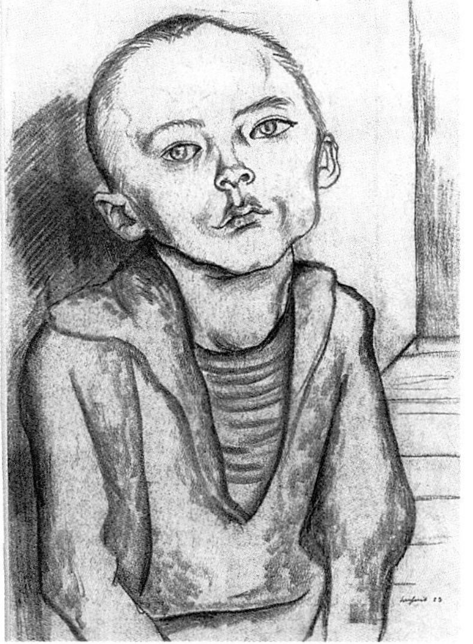

Richard Seewald
Young Girl with Cat (Mädchen mit Katze), 1917 (cat. no. 44)

Bernhard Kretzschmar
Standing Boy (Stehender Knabe), 1921 (cat. no. 27)

Wilhelm Lachnit
Boy in Sailor Suit (Knabe in Matrosenjacke), 1923
(cat. no. 28)

publicity? Involved as it is with the exhibition and commercialization of the self, sentimentalism cannot exist without an audience."[4]

In recent years, however, sentimentality has begun to be reconsidered. In her introduction to *The Culture of Sentiment,* for example, Shirley Samuels has closely analyzed exactly what characterizes nineteenth-century American sentimental literature, and in so doing moves from accusation back to description, a move signaled by the use of the word "sentiment" rather than "sentimentality."[5] Sentiment, Samuels points out, deals in affect and sensuality, often to an excessive degree. Sentiment is a vehicle for nostalgia, for what is lost; it is the language of losers. Sentiment, moreover, allows its audience to accept loss. Sentiment does not deal in agency or in the ability to impose logic, but deals rather in passivity, passivity often pushed to the extreme of pathetic suffering. Politically and socially, sentiment provides a shortcut through controversial issues by simply appealing to empathy and soliciting the viewer's emotional identification. It is an easy way to understand an issue and can reach enormous audiences with very little or no formal training in either art or what art represents. Sentiment is therefore often enlisted to elicit sympathy for the powerless, hence the abolitionist use of sentiment, most famously in the case of Harriet Beecher Stowe's *Uncle Tom's Cabin* (with the figure of a child, little Eva, at its heart).

Sentiment reduces problems from the political or ideological to the personal. In the sentimental work of visual art, the body is the personal. The particular sentimental power of the visual arts is their ability to literally exhibit through the body, to mark emotions with dramatic facial expressions, gestures, and the orchestration of gazes and gestures among figures. Besides exhibiting the effect of emotions on bodies, the sentimental image also engages narrative, implying narrative within the image and linking the image to external narratives. The impact of many sentimental images comes from our projection both backward and forward in time of the causes or consequences of the scene we see. In short, the sentimental image is one that aims to create an effect, not to be self-contained. The sentimental is not an object of contemplation, but an object of empathy and projection, an object which is intended to create an effect on a situation outside itself. The sentimental image is intimately bound up with the circumstances of its audience and its time.

In the nineteenth century, marginally powerful groups used sentiment ostensibly on behalf of less powerful groups. Women, for instance, used sentiment on behalf of slaves. Part of sentimentality's bad reputation comes from a suspicion that it makes spurious claims, acting at least as much to promote the moral status or professional pretensions of its authors as the welfare of what it represents. Women, for instance, specialized in the subject of the child because it was their only safe avenue to professional art careers. Dubious or not, this function of sentiment alerts us that sentiment is about function as well as form. It also alerts us to the fact that the authors of sentiment tend to be motivated by their borderline positions in society and a desire to alter those positions. Shirley Samuels again: "Sentimentality in nineteenth-century America, then, appears not so much a genre as an operation or a set of actions within discursive models of affect and identification that effect connections across gender, race, and class boundaries."[6] To which we might add: across age boundaries. Sentiment may sometimes be a choice among modes of representation, but it is more often the effect, or the consequence, of a social situation. Sentimental pictures of childhood expressed the social concept of Romantic childhood on behalf of the adult class and gender interests it served.

At our moment on the cusp between twentieth and twenty-first centuries, we have a newly clear perspective on sentiment. Just as earlier in our century Modernists refused to accept sentimentality's stylistic and social assumptions, so we now no longer take Modernism for granted. Modernism's formalism has itself almost run its historical course, allowing us to see it as a historically specific competitor of sentimentality, rather than an inherently superior mode of art. The passage of time enables us to see how pictures in this exhibition like Wilhelm Lachnit's 1923 *Boy in Sailor Suit* (cat. no. 28, p. 40), Otto Dix's 1922 *Workers' Children* (cat. no. 15, p. 22), and Rudolf Schlichter's c. 1924-25 *Circus Children* (cat. no. 42, p.22) react against pictures by artists like Frère, Bouguereau, or Sadler as much as, chronologically at least, they superceded them. Martel Schwichtenberg's c. 1920 *Girl in Red Striped Skirt* (cat. no. 43, p. 69), Alice Sommer's 1925 *Two Sisters* (cat. no. 46, p. 40), or Richard Seewald's 1917 *Young Girl with Cat* (cat. no. 44, p. 40) not only replace one esthetic with another, abandoning realism in favor of a progressively more rigorous abstraction, they also react against a mode of perception, by refusing narrative and easy empathy with laconic figure studies and a cult of awkward or even ugly appearances, forcing the viewer away from a picture's connections to its social circumstances and toward the contemplation of pure form. Consider the difference between Sadler's *The Dame's School* and John Quinton Pringle's 1910 *Portrait of a Boy: A Reluctant Subject* (cat. no. 37, p. 25). Both show boys of the same age and type, and in both pictures the boys are not enjoying themselves. But in Sadler's painting, the youth of the boys is part of a story; their fresh faces are contrasted with the woman who fits the stereotype of the mean hard (switch-wielding) spinster schoolteacher. As she points sternly to the globe she purports to teach them geography, but the map behind them shows us that the real future of Britain is the boys themselves. Sadler absorbs viewers in his story, as well as in the many meticulously rendered details of his picture: books, prints, wooden desk,

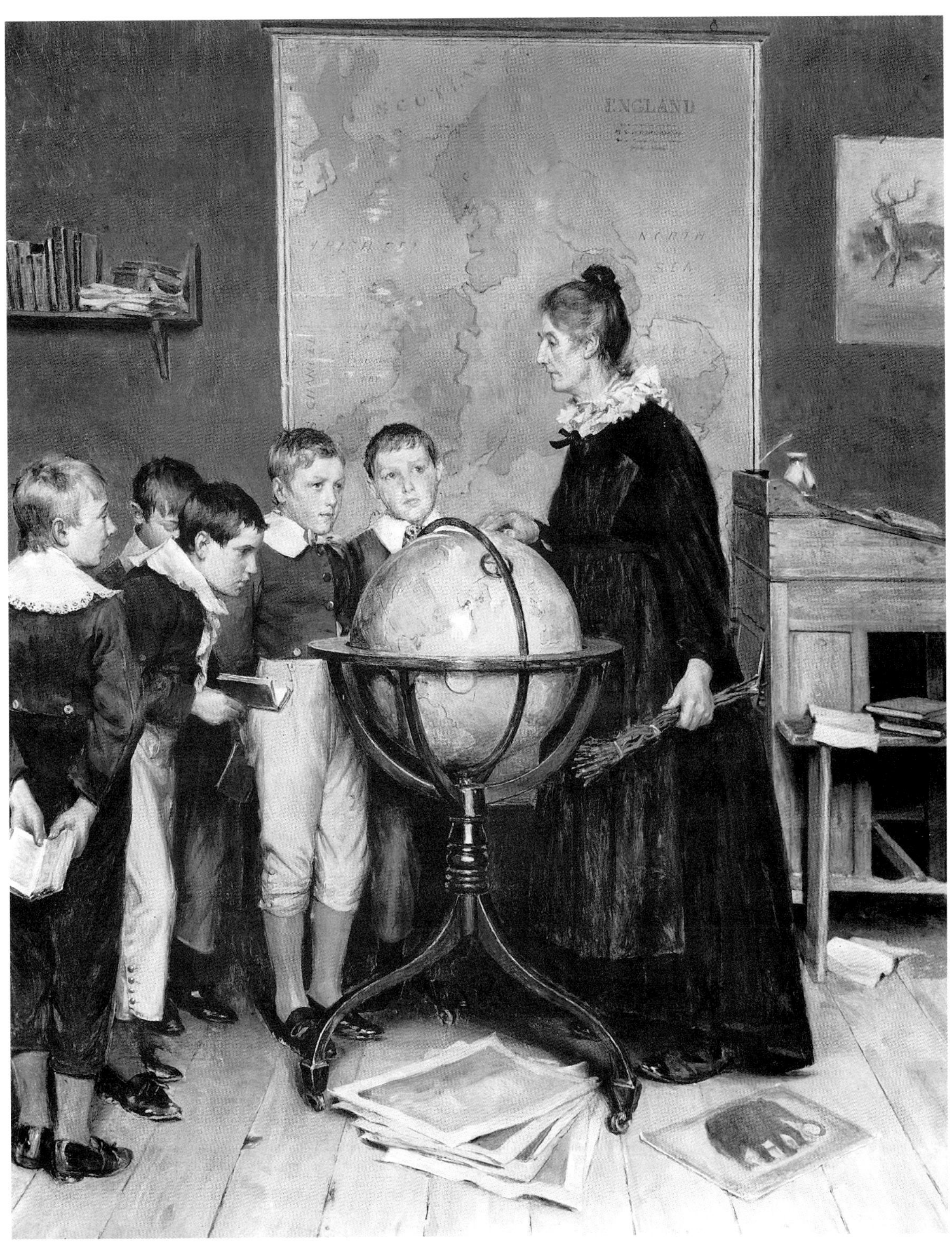

Walter Dendy Sadler
The Dame's School, c. 1900
(cat. no. 41)

gleaming globe, maps, costume, varied facial expressions. Pringle, on the other hand, makes his boy subject opaquely enigmatic. We are given no clues about how or why the boy is a reluctant subject. The artist focuses us instead on his brushwork and on the formal relationship between the volumes of the boy's face in the foreground and the landscape behind him. The Sadler is not only about a lesson, it also intends to teach us a lesson about the history of England, one which we can take satisfaction in having already seen unfold as the picture—painted in about 1900 but set in the first decades of the nineteenth century—(retroactively) predicts. We know doubly what the children in the image are supposed to be innocent of. Pringle teaches us a lesson about color, form, and the transformation of three dimensions into two, or rather, Pringle does not purport to teach us a lesson at all, but rather to provide us with an internally coherent esthetic sensation.

Both Sadler's and Pringle's moments are now past. Our moment is not only one of transition away from a Modernist esthetic, but also away from the Romantic concept of childhood. As we redefine childhood again, feeling that children are more complicated, and more individual, than Romantic ideals suggested, it becomes possible to further reevaluate pictures of children made in the last two centuries. Margaret Cohen, in an important new book on nineteenth-century French sentimental literature, *The Sentimental Education of the Novel,* points out that sentiment may not be the false expression of a political situation, as earlier critics of sentimentality maintained, but rather the accurate representation of a situation whose contradictions or paradoxes it was politically expedient to deny.[7] Sentimentality expresses what Cohen calls the double bind: the impossibility of resolution between conflicting yet enforced rules.

The Romantic concept of childhood was exactly that: a precarious equilibrium between mutually contradictory propositions. The innocence at the heart of Romantic childhood must be an edenic state from which adults fall, never to return. Nor can Romantic children know adults or the adult world; they are by definition unconscious of adult desires, including adults' desire for childhood. The Romantic child is desirable precisely to the extent it does not understand desire. So the image of the Romantic child is supposed to be an unconscious one, one that does not connect with adults, one that seems unaware of adults. Yet the image of that childhood is an exhibition for adults, a presentation of childhood to adults, the transformation of the child into the object of a desiring adult gaze.

Most troublingly, the innocence of the modern Romantic child entails and even provokes adult sexual knowledge. A polar opposition of values is also a binary opposition.
 If one value is defined mainly as the opposite of something else, then perceiving one value

always entails thinking of the other value. In some nineteenth-century genre paintings of children, we now see a disquieting oscillation between innocence and knowledge. In Bouguereau's *Child at Bath,* for instance, the exposure of the child's torso makes us wonder whether the proof of innocence might not be its denial. Is the little girl innately innocent, is she sexy despite her innocence, or is she sexy because of her innocence? In Max Liebermann's 1871 *The Cobbler's Girl* (cat. no. 30, p. 64), the paradoxes of innocence are strained to the limit as a childish gesture of putting a finger in mouth and a childishly direct gaze become simultaneously solicitations of the viewer. The innocent and the coy have merged. In his brave book, *Child-Loving,* James Kincaid argues that Romantic innocence was always an inherently flawed concept.[8] Because the Victorians and Edwardians believed children were categorically different from adults by virtue of their innocence, Kincaid suggests, children seemed other to adults yet better than adults. By being at once other and better, they became irresistibly desirable. Children could only become desirable if they were genuinely believed to be innocent. Innocence itself became the object of desire. This paradoxical desirability of innocence put an irresolvable tension at the core of Romantic childhood. Tension held the whole construction of childhood in place for a while, but by the late twentieth century its difficulties have become apparent. For Kincaid, this difficulty puts all children at risk. Defined as the opposite of adult sexuality, childhood innocence always runs the danger of becoming too alluringly opposite, too enticingly off-limits. The blankness of innocence allows adults to project whatever fantasies they want onto children, whether adoring or abusive. Art historian Marcia Pointon has warned of the particular dangers pictures posed to girls.[9] By likening the girl child to the adult woman, Pointon argues, adult women were infantilized and female children were sexualized. Innocence made girls vulnerable.

Pictures of children resolve these contradictions in the Romantic concept of childhood. At least, they appear to. Cohen reminds us in her work on sentimental novels of Hegel's observation in his *Antigone* that tragedy is the resolution of double binds at the level of the esthetic.[10] Pictures could make all the problems of Romantic childhood seem to disappear. Even the Modernist pictures that react against the sentimentality associated with pictures of childhood only confirm its power, albeit backhandedly. They comment on prevailing ideals, often negatively, and offer us a stylistic alternative to sentiment, but almost never an ideological alternative. Some of the pictures in this exhibition, paying tribute to the power of the Romantic concept, even accommodate advanced Modernist styles to Romantic childhood ideals, in works like Pierre-Auguste Renoir's 1902 *Portrait of Coco* (cat. no. 39, p. 67) or Édouard Vuillard's c. 1904-05 *Child with Ribbons* (cat. no. 55, p. 66), in which a latter-day cupid-cherub plays amid an almost abstract still-life of ribbons.

Some pictures resolve conflicts more compellingly than others. Among the most successful pictures in this regard are those by Mary Cassatt. In works like her c. 1910 *Baby John Asleep, Sucking His Thumb* (cat. no 9, p. 62), she not only reconciles an advanced Impressionist style with sentimental subject matter, but also manages to undo the double bind of the modern maternity so essential to Romantic childhood. The woman who devoted herself to the new child and created the domestic domain within which to form its identity, acceded to her own identity as she lost it, as she became that glorified absence of individuality, the mother. The modern mother is a self who is self-less, the one who must choose all the time, in countless ways, between self-fulfillment and duty to the collective family. In Cassatt's paintings and prints, the mother, though represented as a particular person, is not an autonomous individual. She is literally someone with no boundaries of her own, someone joined physically to her child, merged with the child along zones of physical contact. The space, surface design, and color of her pictures in their entirety are organized around the physical bond between mother and child. Maternity is made both vividly present and yet removed from the present. Maternity does not exist in the real world, except inasmuch as the child is the world. The mother in these images is everything to the child, and nothing to the world. Cassatt turns this double bind into visual pleasure. The moments she represents are moments of pleasure, pictures of the pleasure that mother and baby take in each other. Inventive and elegant composition, sensuous color or printing, the shifting play of light tones, all make Cassatt's pictures themselves pleasures; they offer the viewer esthetics to heighten what they represent. Maybe all babies have to grow up; maybe all mothers have to lose their pleasure in their babies; maybe being a mother means by definition the one who loses her baby; but the picture restores that pleasure; the picture promises maternal pleasure can last forever, if only in the picture. And just in case the moment of one picture cannot make that promise convincingly enough, the image is repeated over and over and over. The mother-child subject, as Cassatt pictured it so many times in the last three decades of her career, is a compulsively repeated collective fantasy, one which only sentimentality could represent. Cassatt's pictures are powerful because of the esthetics of sentimentality, not despite sentimentality.

Only the very exceptional artist could escape dominant ideas about childhood, especially during the nineteenth century. Berthe Morisot did. Her 1888 *Julie Listening* (cat. no. 33, p. 32) is, like Cassatt's late pictures of children, one in a long series. From the time of her daughter Julie's birth in 1879 until her own death in 1895, Morisot devoted herself mostly to representing her child. Impressionism urged her both to be modern and to heed her own personal experience. In her pictures, the child does grow up and away from the mother, all the while maintaining a close bond to her parent. In Morisot's pictures, that bond is an intellectual and artistic one, as Julie's involvement with music—whether listening to the piano or playing the violin herself—mirrors her mother's involvement in painting. More than aware of her mother's project, Julie collaborates with it. Artist and model, mother and daughter together create another kind of image of childhood, one which would remain virtually unique until late in the twentieth century.

Notes

1. Leo Steinberg, *The Sexuality of Christ in Renaissance Art and in Modern Oblivion,* 2nd ed. (Chicago: University of Chicago Press, 1996).
2. Philippe Ariès, *Centuries of Childhood: A Social History of Family Life,* trans. Robert Baldick (New York: Knopf, 1962).
3. Martha Frick Symington Sanger, *Henry Clay Frick: An Intimate Portrait* (New York: Abbeville Press, 1998).
4. Ann Douglas, *The Feminization of American Culture* (New York: Knopf, 1977), p. 254.
5. Shirley Samuels, ed., *The Culture of Sentiment: Race, Gender, and Sentimentality in Nineteenth-Century America* (New York and Oxford: Oxford University Press, 1992).
6. Samuels, *The Culture of Sentiment,* p. 6.
7. Margaret Cohen, *The Sentimental Education of the Novel* (Princeton, N. J.: Princeton University Press, 1999).
8. James R. Kincaid, *Child-Loving: The Erotic Child and Victorian Culture* (New York and London: Routledge, 1992).
9. Marcia Pointon, "The State of a Child," in *Hanging the Head: Portraiture and Social Formation in Eighteenth-Century England* (New Haven and London: Yale University Press, 1993), pp. 177-226.
10. Cohen, *The Sentimental Education of the Novel.*

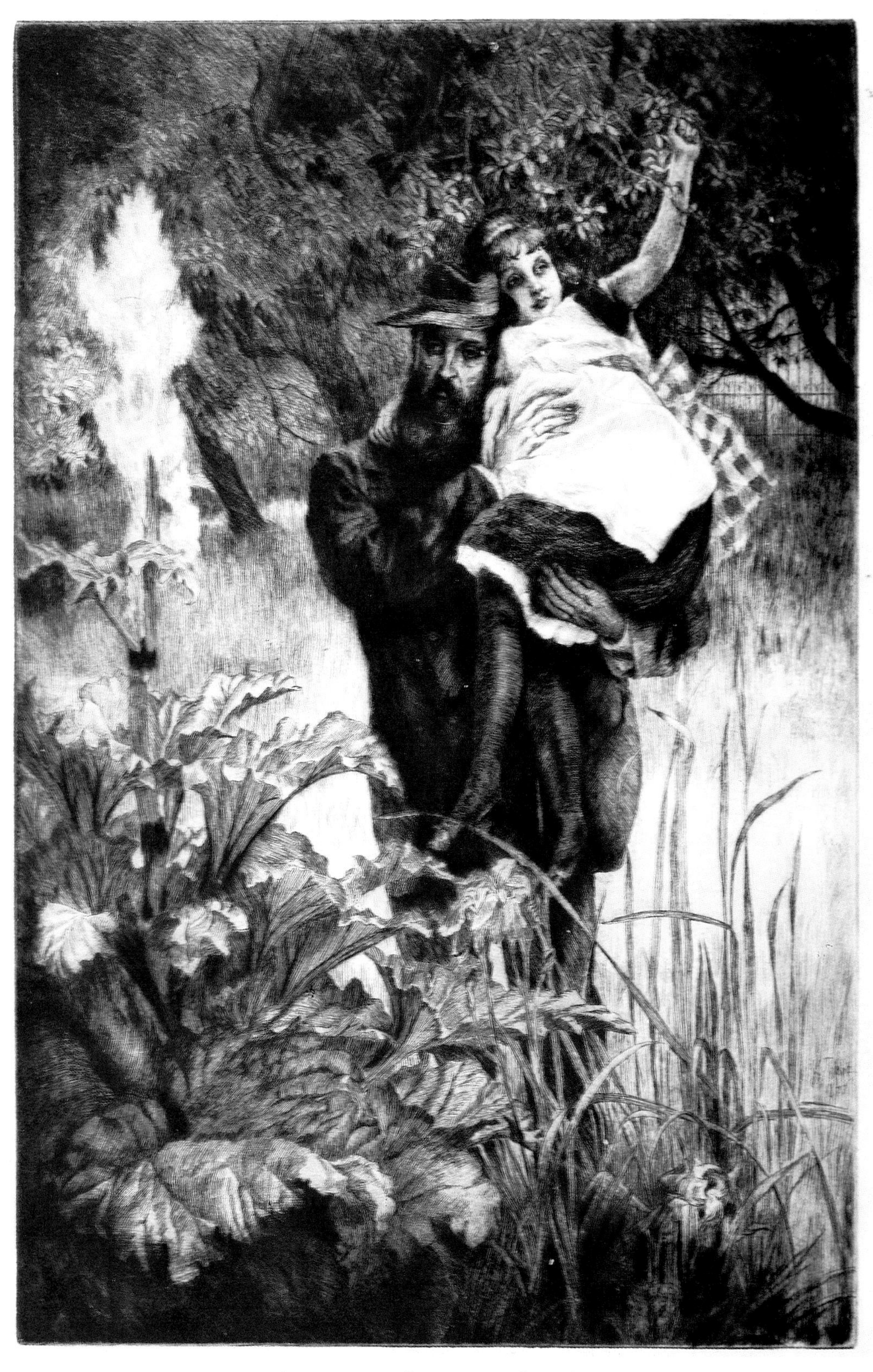

James (Jacques-Joseph) Tissot, *The Widower (Le veuf)*, 1877 (cat. no. 51)

A Century of Contradictions: Images of Children in History and in Art

James Marten

"One of the puzzles of our history," writes the historian C. John Sommerville, "is the fact that the greatest exploitation of children coincided with the greatest glorification of childhood."[1] Sommerville is referring to the latter half of the nineteenth century, when child labor helped propel the industrial revolution at the same time that sentimental notions of children dominated child-rearing guides, literature, and artistic representations of childhood. Indeed, competing images of children and of childhood filled the cultural landscape of western Europe and the United States between the middle of the nineteenth and the middle of the twentieth centuries. As Americans and Europeans witnessed decades of breathtaking economic growth and crushing economic hardship, of acquiring and losing colonies all over the world, of exhilarating social progress and alarming poverty, the lives of their children varied widely. At the same time that millions of children, many under the age of ten, labored in coal mines and sweatshops, as newsboys and bobbin girls, the economic boom their sweat and blood helped to fuel allowed the offspring of the upper and middle classes to enjoy an extended childhood and youth unburdened by responsibility, attend school for longer periods of time, and surround themselves with mountains of commercially manufactured toys and games. In this version of childhood, youngsters were innocents whose parents insisted on shielding them from the outside world, from the corruption and politics and ambivalent morality of the urbanizing, industrializing west. At least that was the ideal that dominated representations of childhood.

Of course, any reader of the novels of Charles Dickens, of any major urban newspaper, or of the alarming reports issued by "child saving" reform organizations, knows that many—most—nineteenth-century children did not participate in this idealized childhood. Vast communities of poverty-stricken laborers and their families filled the immigrant ghettoes of New York and the slums of London, Edinburgh, and Paris. There, children were compelled to supplement their parents' meager wages, were exposed to the vice and corruption bred by poverty and overcrowding, and grew up much faster than their clean-scrubbed, affluent peers. No one could describe their grim lives, bound by necessity, as "innocent," and their experiences would eventually be acknowledged. As the decades passed, moreover, Freud's emphasis on subconscious desires in human beings at very young ages shocked westerners into looking at children differently. In addition, post-1900 political developments such as nationalism and Fascism incorporated children into the adults' political world, and the separate culture formed among increasingly independent youth forged even greater threats to the innocence of childhood in most industrialized nations.

Naturally, the tension between the idealized version of childhood and its less positive parallels surfaced in artistic images of children rendered between the 1850s and the 1950s. In one sense, the artists' subjects reflect the notion of childhood as a kind of pastoral period through which the luckiest children passed on their way to middle-class adulthood; many children did live such lives—especially the children of the patrons most likely to purchase paintings chronicling those happy times—and, as such, those pictures document historical reality. On the other hand, as the grinding poverty in which many children lived was "discovered" by reformers and artists alike, those rosy images became ironic examples of excess, balanced by far less optimistic portrayals of children and youth. Finally, as the world was warped by imperialism, depression, racial conflict, and war in the twentieth century, artists seemed to accept that, like adults, children were often exposed to the more sinister aspects of modern life. The paintings that appear in *Children in Art,* then, reflect the contradictory forces acting on the lives of children.

Historians have debated for decades when Europeans and Americans began to consider childhood as a separate phase of life. Some historians have argued that before the seventeenth century there was no concept of childhood, and that detachment and even brutality characterized parents' relationships with their sons and daughters, while some recent studies have been more sympathetic to earlier generations of parents.[2] It seems clear, however, that by the mid-nineteenth century, notions of childhood and of child rearing had appeared that seem relatively modern, at least compared to the rather uncompromising disciplinary and spiritual attitudes projected by seventeenth- and eighteenth-century American and European Protestants. The argument against the idea that children were the root of all evil—a notion commonly but a bit unfairly attributed to the Puritans—can be traced to the 1762 publication *of Émile,* a path-breaking work on child nurturing by Jean-Jacques Rousseau, which opened with the simple declaration that "The Author of Nature makes all things good; man meddles with them and they become evil." Rousseau's naturalistic approach to the education and development of children, free of the strait-jacket of narrow discipline and overly formal education and embracing more loving relationships between parents and their children, influenced parents, educators, and reformers for decades to come—although the "unnatural" and rigorous training and rearing of children would continue as well.[3] Rousseau's primary contribution, in the long run, was less to shape the nature of how children were raised than to help spur the sentimentalization of childhood. William Blake's *Songs of Innocence* (1789) and the paintings of children produced by Joshua Reynolds represented this new fascination among artists with the instinctive goodness and innocence of children, which reached its peak in the late Victorian age. Frederick Waugh's *The Artist's Family at Home,* 1887 (cat. no. 57, p. 61) offers a snug image of how Victorian adults also raised family life to the level of a near obsession as they crowded their parlors with symbols of the good life: popular art, overstuffed furniture, family portraits, and pianos. They poured affection onto their children and filled nurseries with the vast assortment of the commercially produced toys and books available by the mid-nineteenth century, many of which appeared in paintings of glowing children and happy families.[4] The innocence attached to nineteenth-century children also came out in the clothes worn by babies, toddlers, and small children of both genders: petticoats and white pantaloons were appropriate for boys and girls alike, as were long curls or, for that matter, short hair. Their androgynous appearance, according to one historian, "became popular not only because it protected a child's ignorance about sex but also because it created an image of innocence that charmed and reassured parents."[5]

The literature produced for children during this period also encouraged the development of highly moralistic, pious, and innocent traits. In the United States, stories and articles in such magazines as *Youth's Companion, Little Pilgrim,* and *Our Young Folks* promoted the principles of hard work, obedience, generosity, humility, and piety; provided moral guidance and examples of the consequences of bad behavior; stressed the importance of family cohesion and of social order; and furnished mild adventure stories, innocent entertainment, and instruction. The values presented in such publications spoke to the notion that children were naturally good, and that that goodness, as they grew older, could be maintained with proper stimulation and care.[6] Sommerville refers to the lessons found in children's literature on both sides of the Atlantic as "the myth of childhood goodness"; it exerted a great power over adults as well as children. The former regarded children as "guardians of virtue" and frequently refused to admit that children could ever behave in reprehensible ways. Even temporarily naughty children—those who got their clothes dirty, teased their pets, illicitly climbed trees, or spoke rudely to servants—seemed to authors of such books and stories to be mischievously precious rather than bad.[7]

By the turn of the twentieth century, however, even in popular culture, western adults were finally realizing that not all children lived these cozy, idealized lives. They had known it before, of course; the response to the deaths and injuries of countless working children in England early in the nineteenth century had been the passage of impossible-to-enforce laws protecting child laborers and the formation of such organizations as the Society for Superseding the Necessity of Climbing Boys. "Child savers" had been rescuing children from poverty in America's big cities since the 1850s, when the Children's Aid Society began transporting children to the ostensibly happier farm families and healthier environments of the western states. But late-nineteenth- and early-twentieth-century reformers added changing perceptions of children to their traditional concern for their virtue.

It had become obvious by that time that many children were neither good nor innocent. Of course, middle-class reformers assumed that most of these paradigm changing youths came from the less privileged classes, but it should have been clear to them that popular culture had moved beyond the "niceness" of earlier forms. In America, although moralistic and wholesome literature for children continued to be published, young readers were increasingly drawn to lurid "dime novels" whose plots featured frontier violence and urban crime and whose characters demonstrated admirable qualities in only superficial ways. Even cheaper "penny dreadfuls" lured English children to stories in which few worthy lessons could be learned. English and American children patronized bawdy vaudeville shows in smoky music halls, and when nickelodeons and, later, movie theaters began showing boxing matches, western shoot 'em ups, and seminude dancers, the moral corruption of American and European youth seemed imminent.[8]

That many children experienced lives far removed from the old ideal was clearly on the minds of members of the English Parliament by the end of Victoria's reign. Beginning with the Prevention of Cruelty to Children Act in 1889, the English government put into operation over the course of the next half century a number of child-related programs that reflected the extent to which the public had accepted the fact that many—most, in some societies—children did not share in the perfect childhood. These programs included plans to improve the health and diet of schoolchildren, created a separate justice system for juvenile defendants (the first juvenile courts in the United States had appeared in 1899), and, just after the Second World War, established local Children's Departments that would oversee the treatment and care of abused, neglected, and otherwise disadvantaged children.[9]

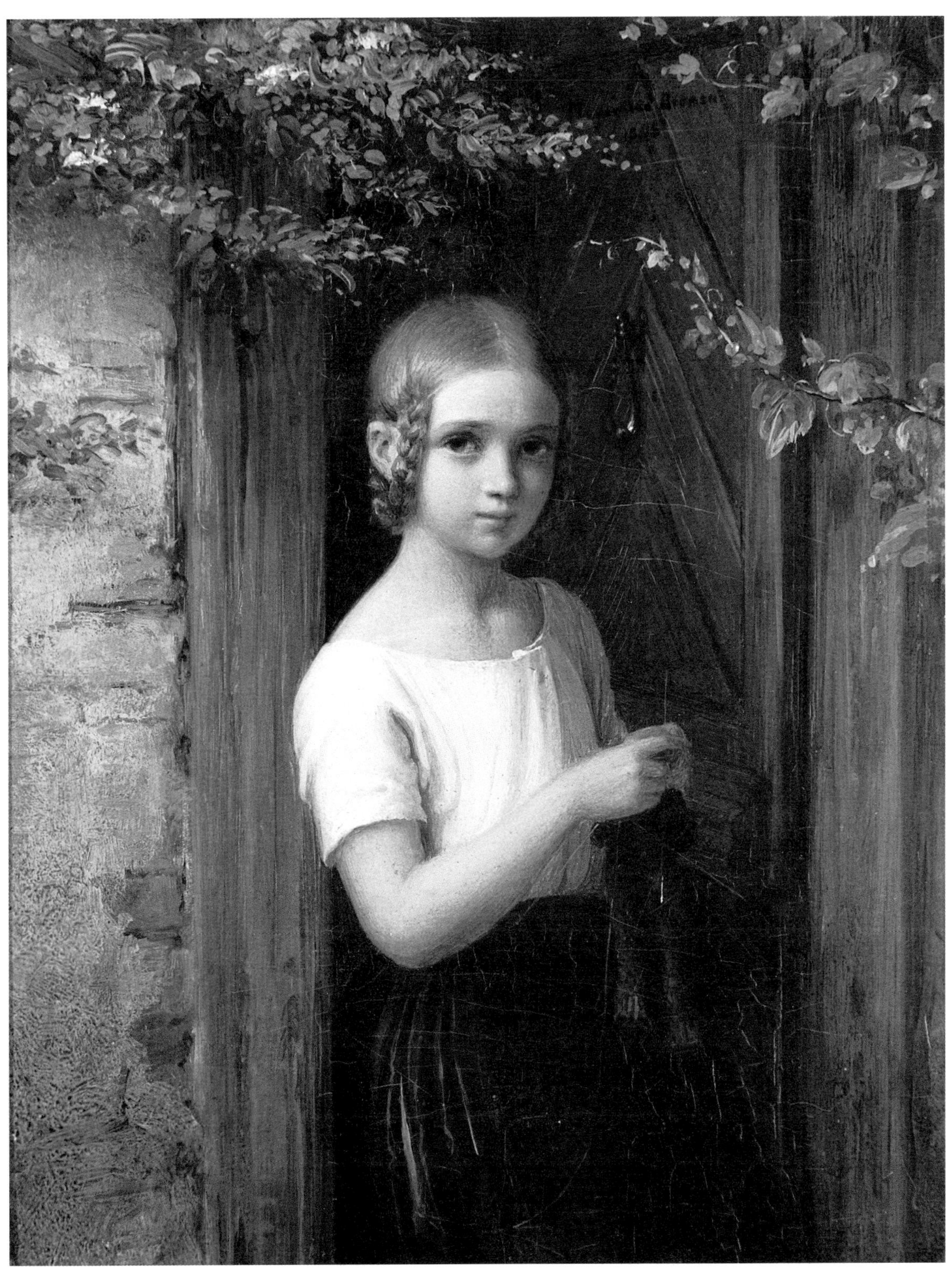

Johann Georg Meyer, called Meyer von Bremen
Girl with Knitting (Ein strickendes Mädchen), 1846 (cat. no. 32)

Ideas regarding children, not coincidentally, also underwent several important changes. American scientists began to publish articles and books in which they expressed their concern that the mounting vices of adult society would eventually drown the supposed goodness of its children. "Each generation," writes Karen Calvert, "seemed to produce fewer geniuses and heroes than the one before." The nineteenth-century belief in progress and the ultimate perfectibility of mankind—encouraged by and reflected in attitudes regarding children—was overshadowed by a grim fear that American society was in the process of degeneration.[10] The arguments of a number of social scientists and biologists also wore away the shine of childhood for many westerners. Charles Darwin had opened the doors to a more scientific study of human behavior, including children; in fact, he published a study of his own toddler's development, in which he often compared the little boy's development to that of wild animals. This may have made adults accustomed to thinking of children more as earthbound angels than as small monkeys uncomfortable, but the scientist who sparked even more controversy was, of course, Freud.

The father of psychoanalysis hardly set out to show that children were depraved beings, but when he published articles with names like "Infant Sexuality" and linked certain childhood behaviors to sexual urges, his "views seemed the height of perversion." Yet within a few years they became an important part of the twentieth-century vocabulary on children. In addition, just after the turn of the century, an American psychologist, Stanley Hall, rather depressingly appraised modern society as being particularly dangerous to the values and character of adolescents. "New dangers threaten all sides," he wrote in 1904 of youngsters' ascent to adolescence, and if teenagers failed to surmount these psychological and moral challenges, they would almost certainly be exposed to "retrogression, degeneracy, or fall."[11] Four decades later, Raphael Soyer's *Portrait of a Young Girl,* c. 1946 (cat. no. 49, p. 81) showed the kind of self-contained but vulnerable teenager that Hall may have been talking about.

By 1900, no rational adult could believe that most children experienced pristine, happy, innocent childhoods—if they had ever believed that. A jarring juxtaposition of these conflicting attitudes appears in some of the scenes in the exhibition. Mary Cassatt's picture of a mother cradling a sleeping infant (*Baby John Asleep, Sucking His Thumb;* cat. no. 9, p. 62) appeared around 1910, the same year that John Quinton Pringle painted his portrait of a disconcertingly knowing boy (*Portrait of a Boy: A Reluctant Subject;* cat. no. 37, p. 25). And, as entertainment venues multiplied, and with them the opportunities to see crime, violence, and sex glorified on the silver screen; as, despite adoption of stricter school attendance mandates by most western countries, children remained important cogs in the industrial machine (exposed brilliantly in the United States by the photographers Jacob Riis in the 1890s and Lewis Hines in the next century); and, as the middle-class family glorified in the nineteenth century found itself battered by economic, social, and political forces, the likelihood that children could be perceived within the old framework of innocence grew smaller and smaller. Indeed, the chronological sweep of this exhibition is capped by Jacob Lawrence's knowing image of the birth of a baby whose mother seemingly turns away from her child in bitter regret (*Birth*, 1948; cat. no. 29, p. 28).

Nothing brought that point home more dramatically than the Second World War. For instance, after they came to power in Germany in the early 1930s, the Nazis incorporated children into the fascist world view, with its extreme nationalism; although nations had for generations sought to socialize and politicize their children through schools and literature—American educators facing the influx into urban schools of millions of Jewish, Polish, and Italian immigrants between the 1880s and the 1920s became agents of Americanization—but the popularity and success of such programs as the Hitler Youth had horrifying consequences. In addition, in unprecedented numbers, children became victims of the war that the Nazis helped spawn: they perished when German bombs fell on London and when British pilots fire-bombed Dresden, when Nanking and Shanghai fell to the Japanese and when nuclear death consumed Hiroshima and Nagasaki. Most appallingly, perhaps, they were among the millions of Jews, Gypsies, and other eastern Europeans sucked into the nightmare that was the holocaust. Remarkably, even as they waited for the gas chambers, Jewish children tried to make sense out of their surroundings by playing games like "Returning the Clothing of the Dead" and "Roll Call." By that time, their "innocent" play reflected the cruelest of ironies.[12]

It is a fallacy to suppose that childhood has been more or less innocent in any given period of time; it is more useful to assume that there have always been countless styles and qualities of lives being led by the youngest members of society. Even though the gap between those children with the greatest wealth and the most opportunities has continued to widen over the last century and a half, the percentage of children living in relative comfort has, in most western countries, grown. Even as our movie screens are filled with streetwise and sexually promiscuous boys and girls who are children in age only, a sense of the old innocence is maintained in the revival of Walt Disney movies, the "American Girl" books and activity series, and even the domestication of Las Vegas with more family-oriented entertainment. Still, as the artists presented in this exhibition show, childhood remains a complex state of being subject to many different interpretations.

Notes

1. C. John Sommerville, *The Rise and Fall of Childhood,* rev. ed. (New York: Vintage, 1990), p. 188.
2. See, for example, Philippe Ariès, *Centuries of Childhood: A Social History of Family Life,* trans. Robert Baldick (New York: Knopf, 1962); Lloyd de Mause, ed., *The History of Childhood* (New York: Psychohistory Press, 1974); and Lawrence Stone, *The Family, Sex and Marriage in England, 1500-1800* (New York: Harper and Row, 1977). Linda Pollock is highly critical of her colleagues' negative portrayals of childrearing; see *Forgotten Children: Parent-Child Relations from 1500 to 1900* (Cambridge: Cambridge University Press, 1983).
3. Sommerville, *The Rise and Fall of Childhood,* pp. 149-54.
4. See, for example, Steven Mintz, *A Prison of Expectations: The Family in Victorian Culture* (New York: New York University Press, 1983).
5. Karen Calvert, *Children in the House: The Material Culture of Early Childhood, 1600-1900* (Boston: Northeastern University Press, 1992), p. 103.
6. Anne Scott MacLeod, *A Moral Tale: Children's Fiction and American Culture, 1820-1860* (Hamden, Conn.: Archon Books, 1975), 104-116; R. Gordon Kelly, *Mother Was a Lady: Self and Society in Selected American Periodicals, 1865-1890* (Westport: Greenwood Press, 1974), p. 4.
7. Sommerville, *The Rise and Fall of Childhood,* pp. 204-6.
8. Harry Hedrick, *Children, Childhood and English Society, 1880-1990* (Cambridge: Cambridge University Press, 1997), pp. 85-87.
9. Hedrick, *Children, Childhood and English Society,* pp. 45-55.
10. Calvert, *Children in the House,* pp. 138-39.
11. Sommerville, *The Rise and Fall of Childhood,* pp. 248-50, 254-55, 240-41.
12. George Eisen, *Children and Play in the Holocaust: Games among the Shadows* (Amherst: University of Massachusetts Press, 1988).

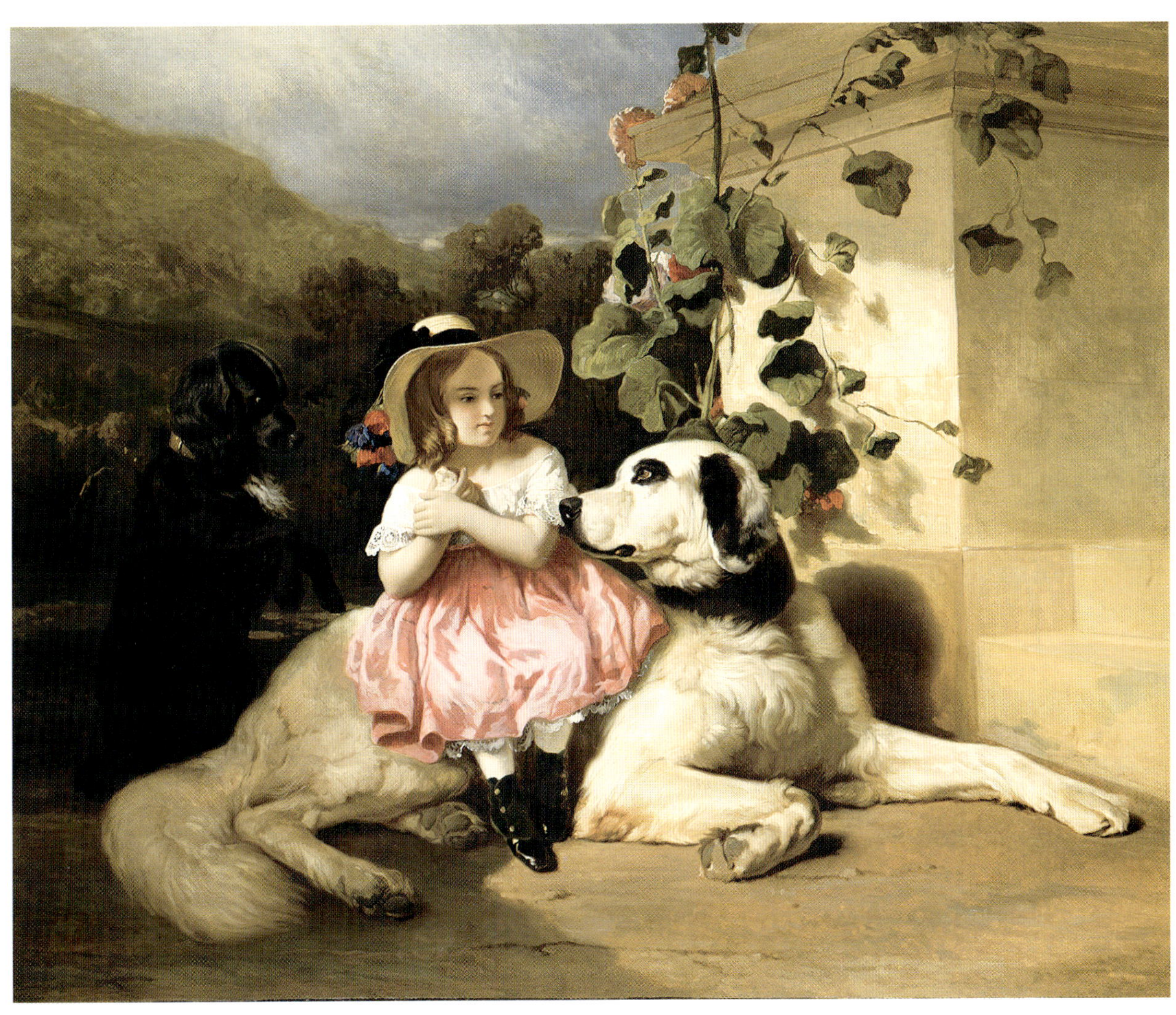

Alfred De Dreux
Innocence between Two Thieves (L'Innocence entre deux larrons), c. 1859
(cat. no. 12)

Pierre Edouard Frere
Young Admiral (Le jeune admiral), c. 1860
(cat. no. 17)

Playing Mother (Jouant maman), 1865
(cat. no. 18)

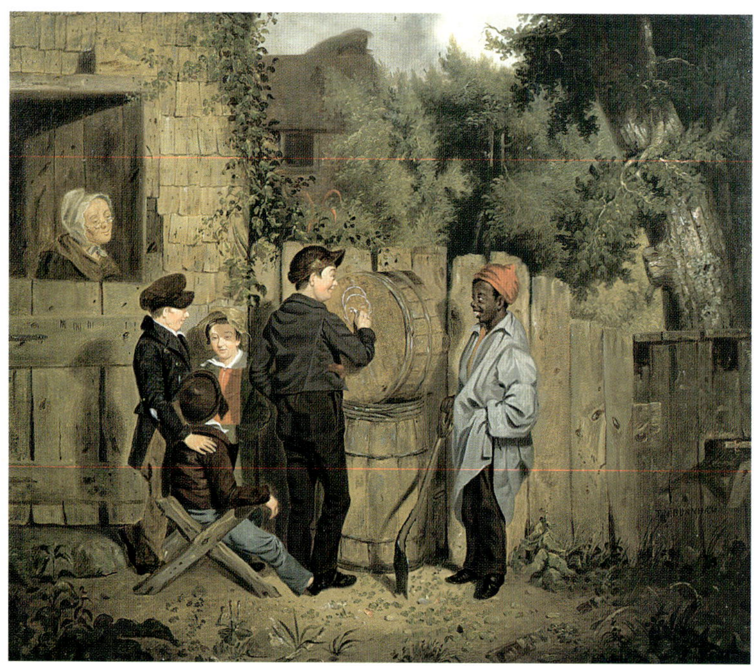

Thomas Mickell Burnham
The Young Artist, 1840
(cat. no. 7)

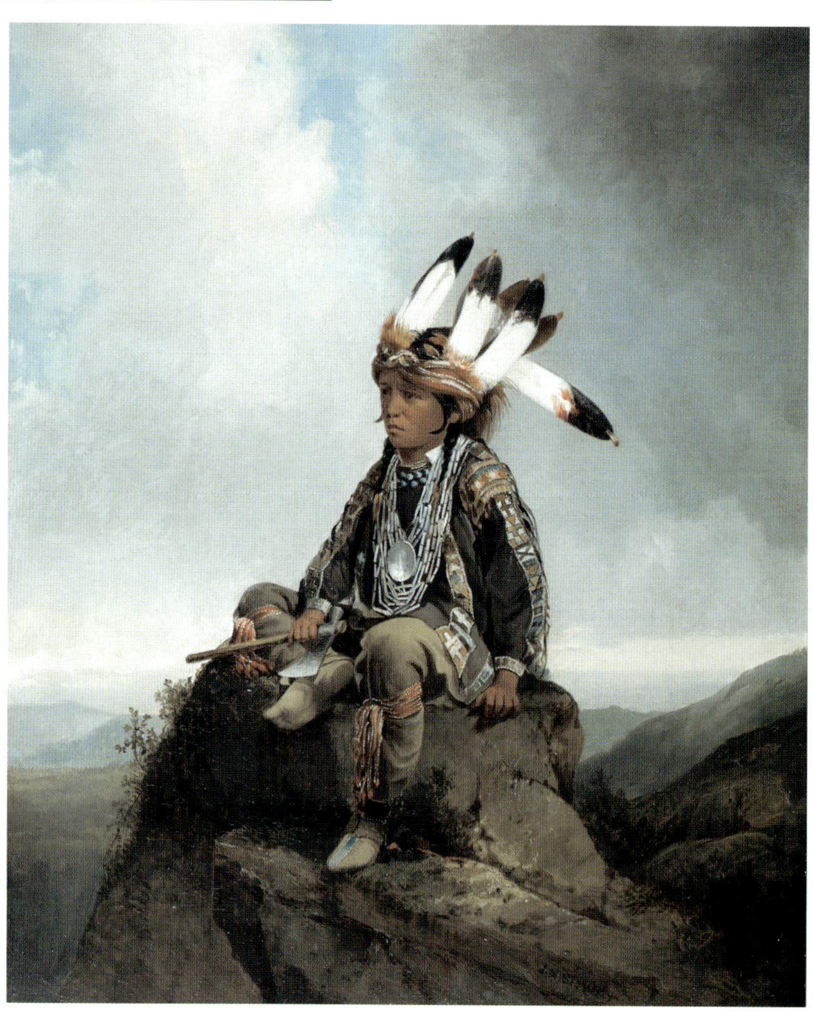

John Mix Stanley
Young Chief Uncas
(cat. no. 50)

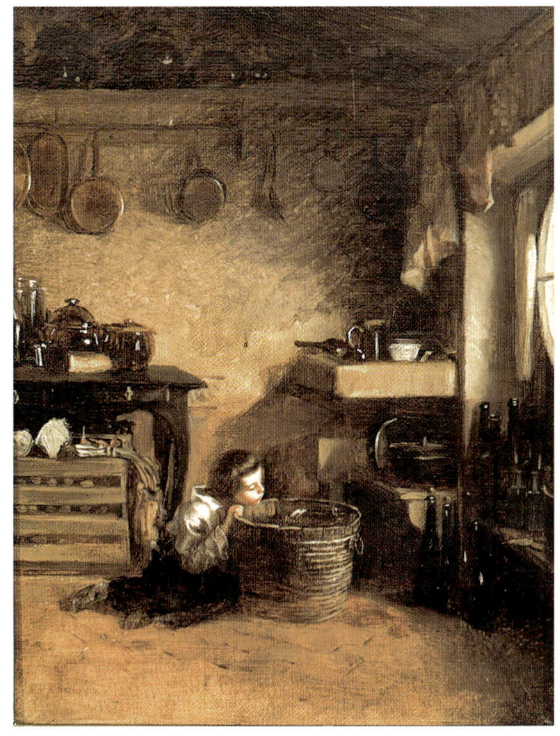

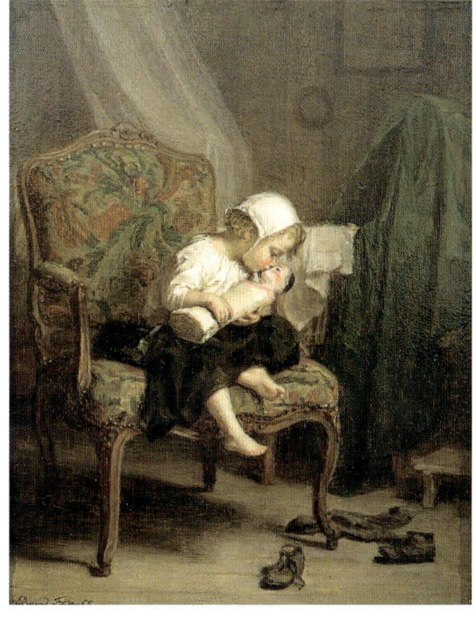

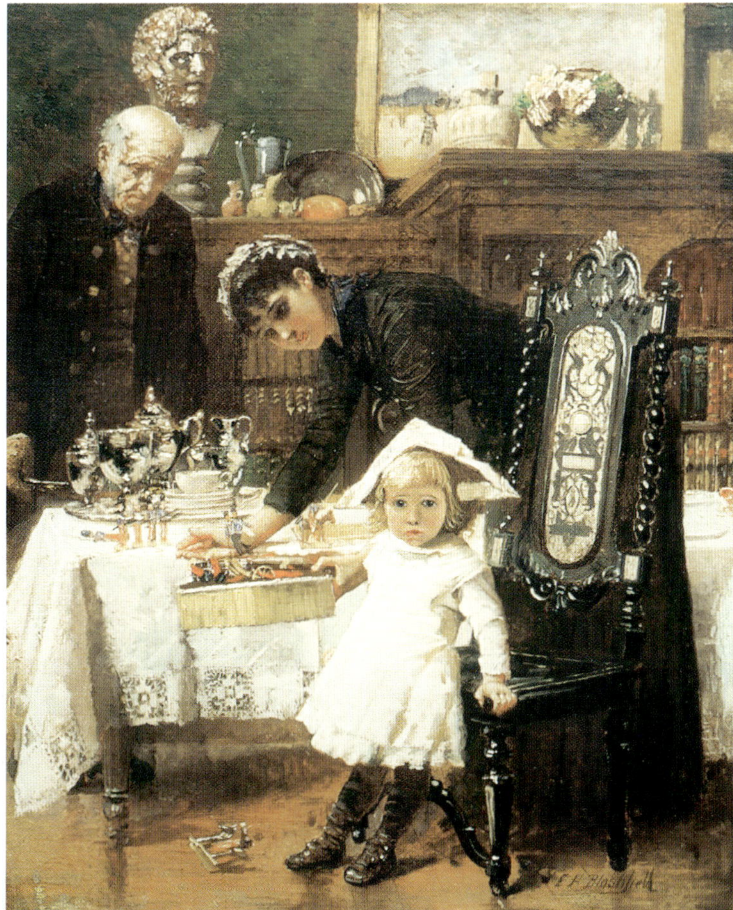

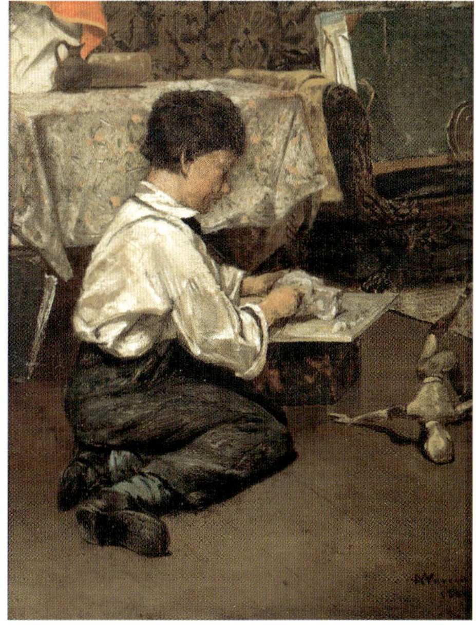

Andrew W. Warren
Clay Modeling, c. 1866
(cat. no. 56)

Edwin Howland Blashfield
Waterloo: Total Defeat, 1882
(cat. no. 2)

John George Brown
Eating the Profits, 1878
(cat. no. 4)

Eyre Crowe
Boys of Blue Coat School, 1877
(cat. no. 11)

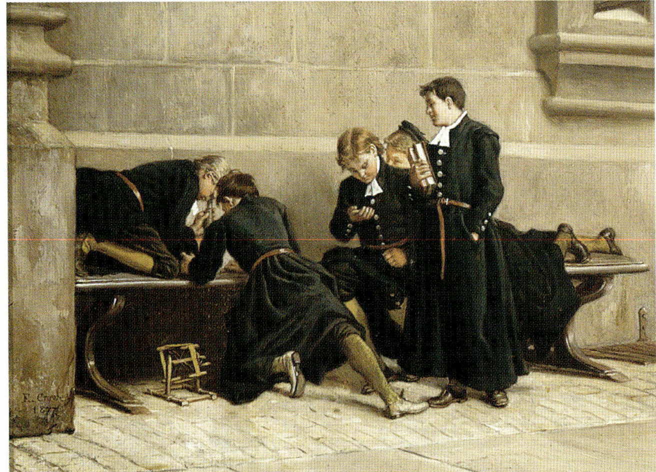

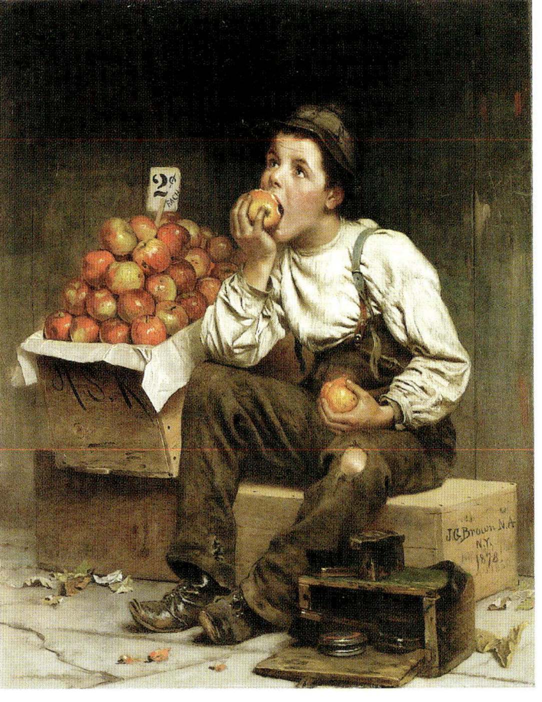

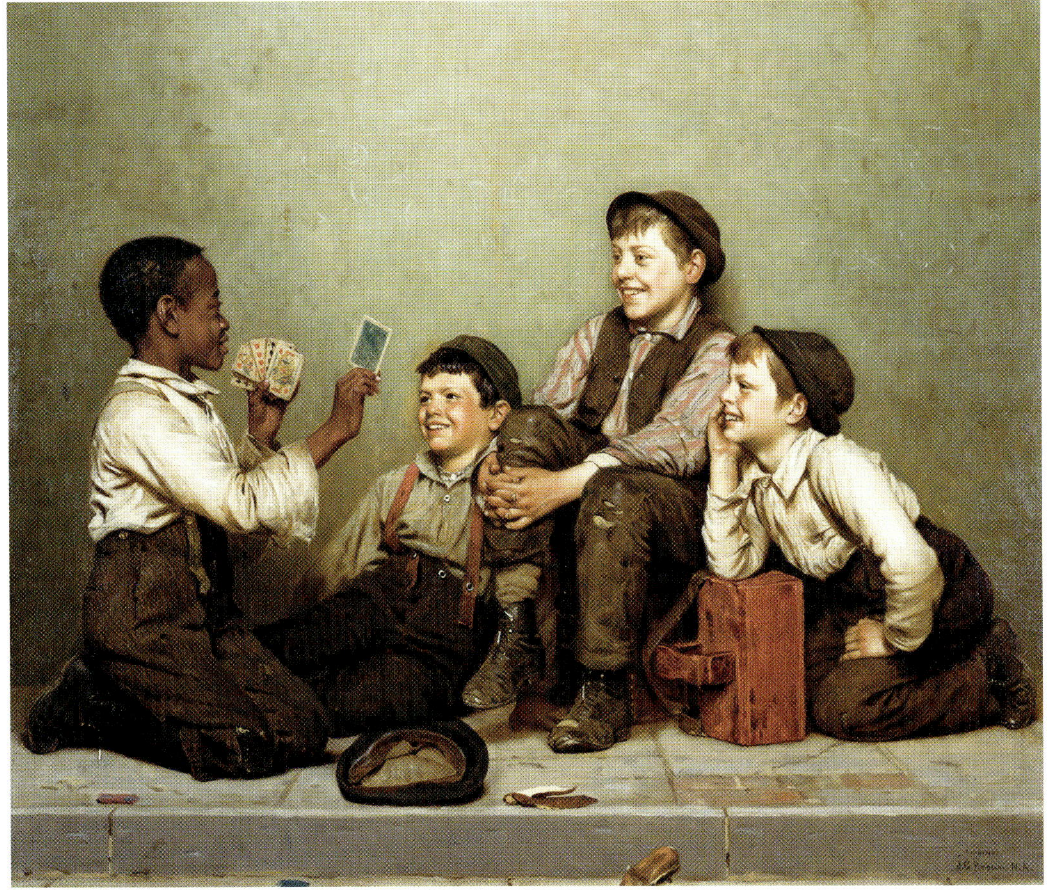

John George Brown, *The Card Trick*, c. 1880s (cat. no. 5)

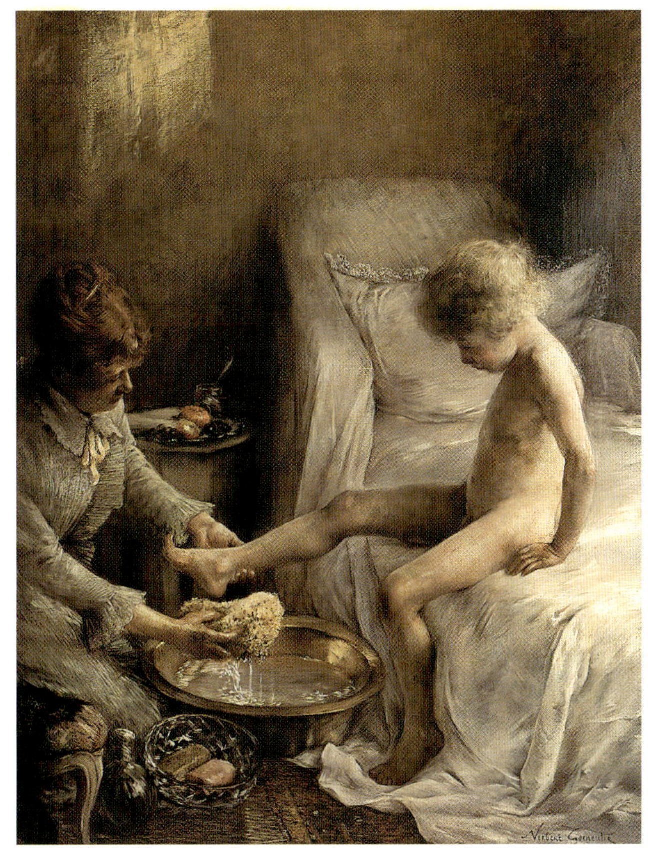

Norbert Goeneutte
Reine Goeneutte Washing the Young Jean Geurard in the Artist's Studio, 1889
(cat. no. 20)

Frederick Judd Waugh
The Artist's Family at Home, 1887
(cat. no. 57)

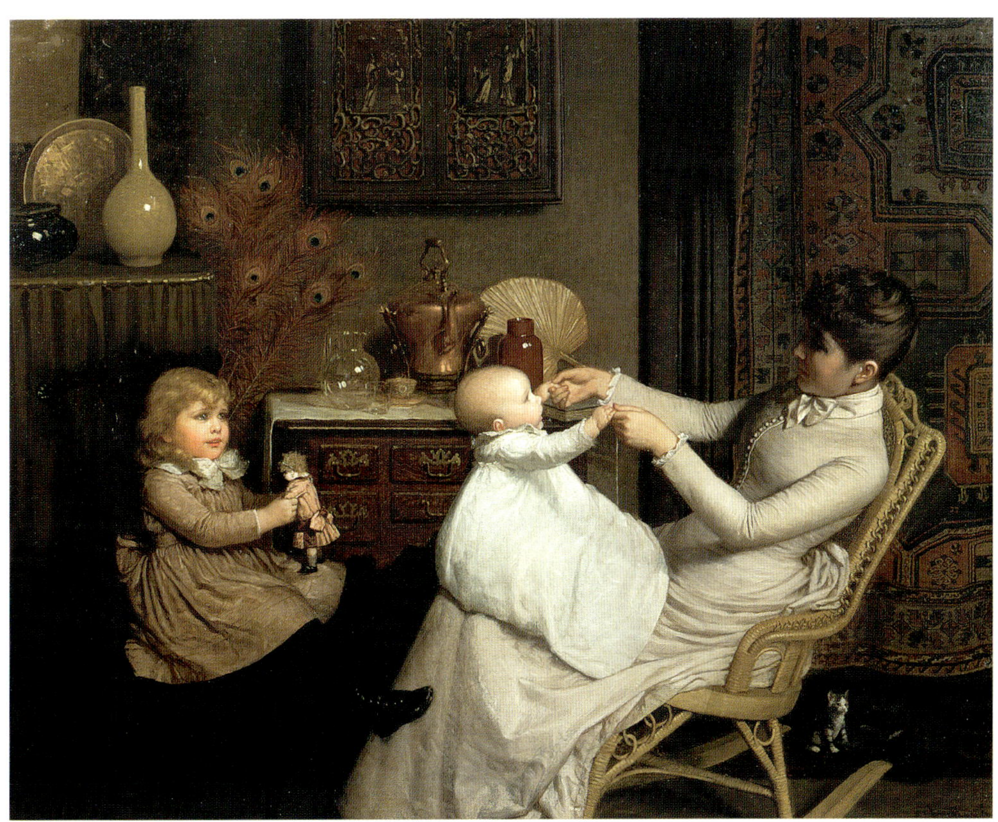

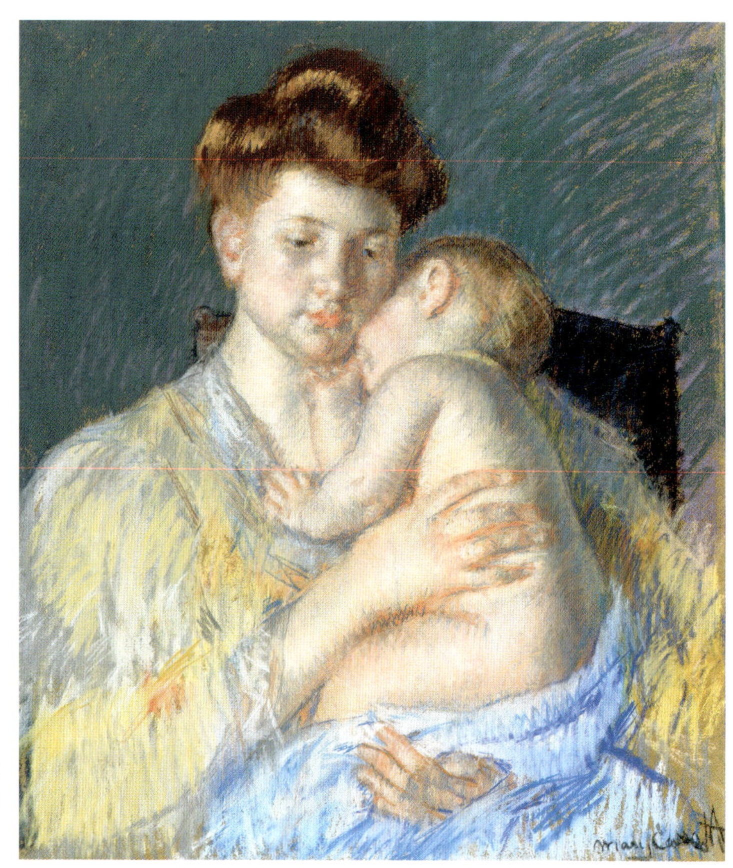

Mary Cassatt
Baby John Asleep, Sucking His Thumb, c. 1910
(cat. no. 9)

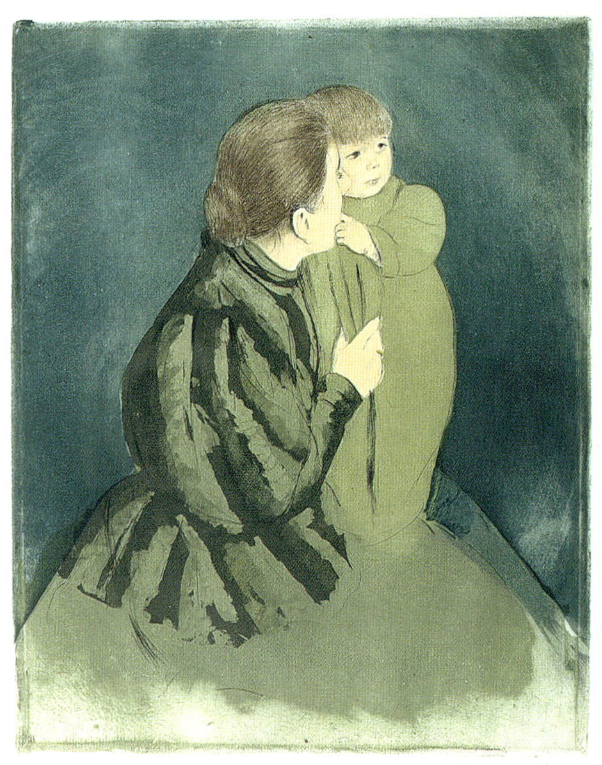

Mary Cassatt
Peasant Mother and Child, c. 1894
(cat. no. 8)

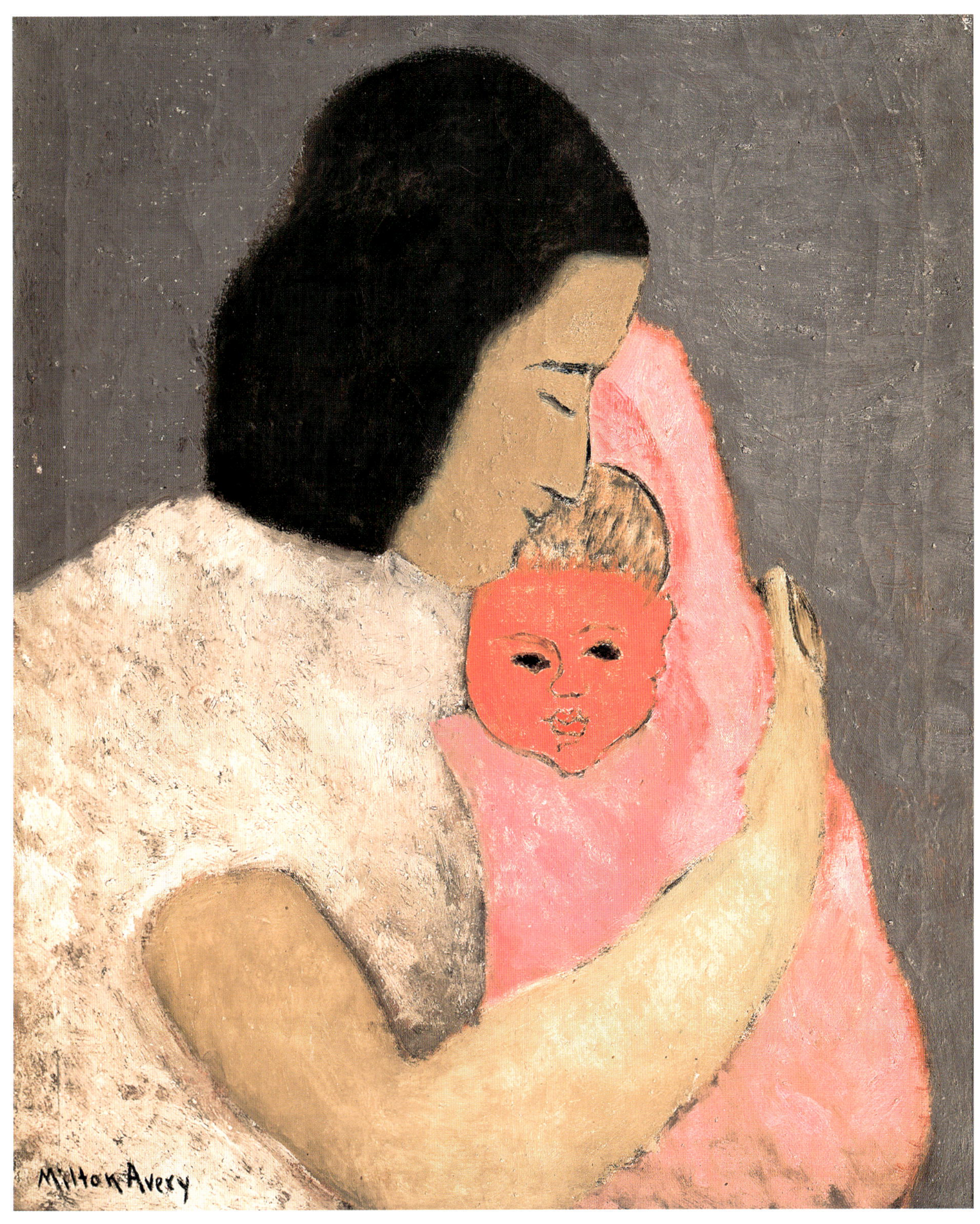

Milton Avery
Maternity, 1933
(cat. no. 1)

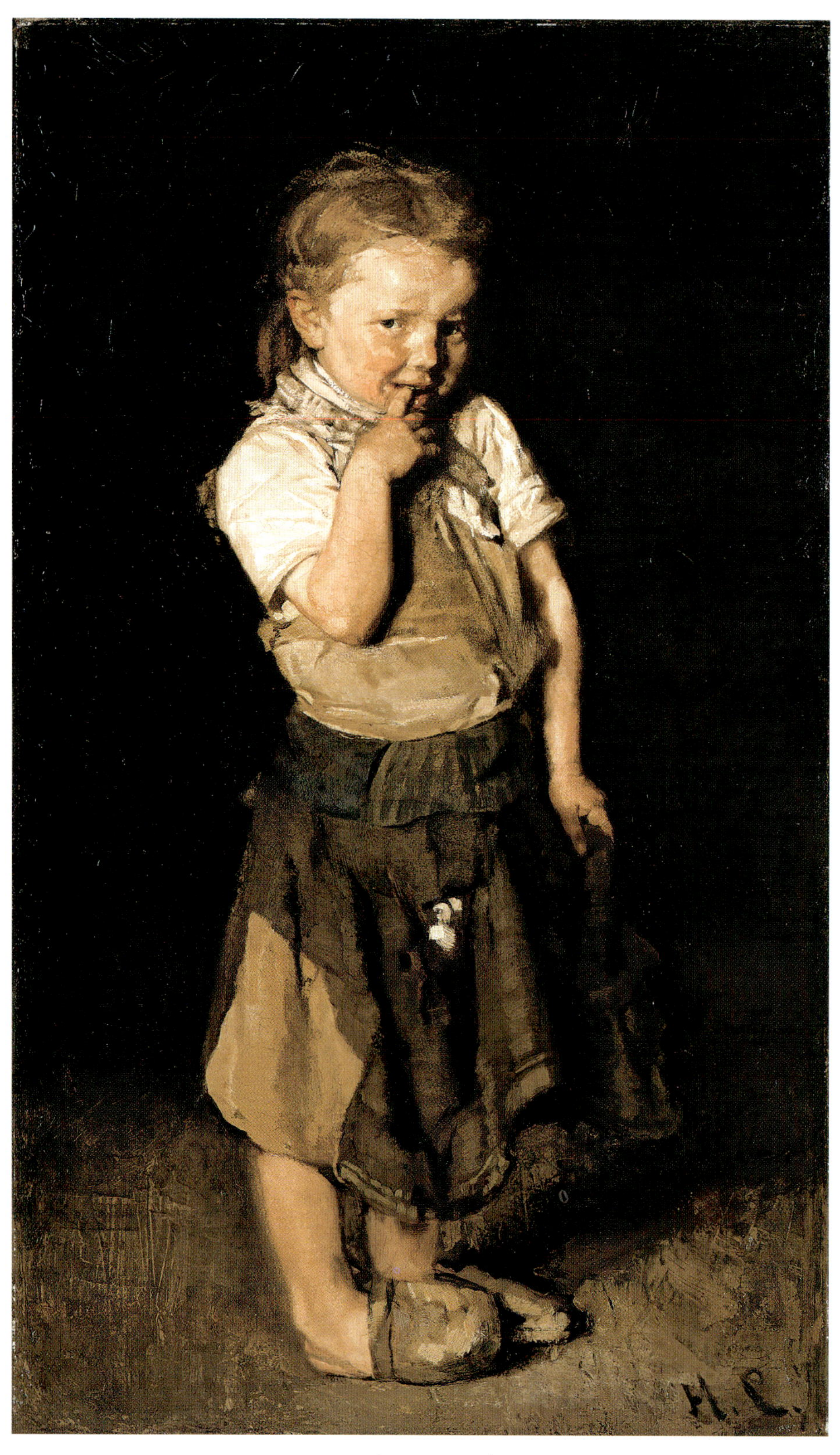

Max Liebermann, *The Cobbler's Girl,* 1871 (cat. no. 30)

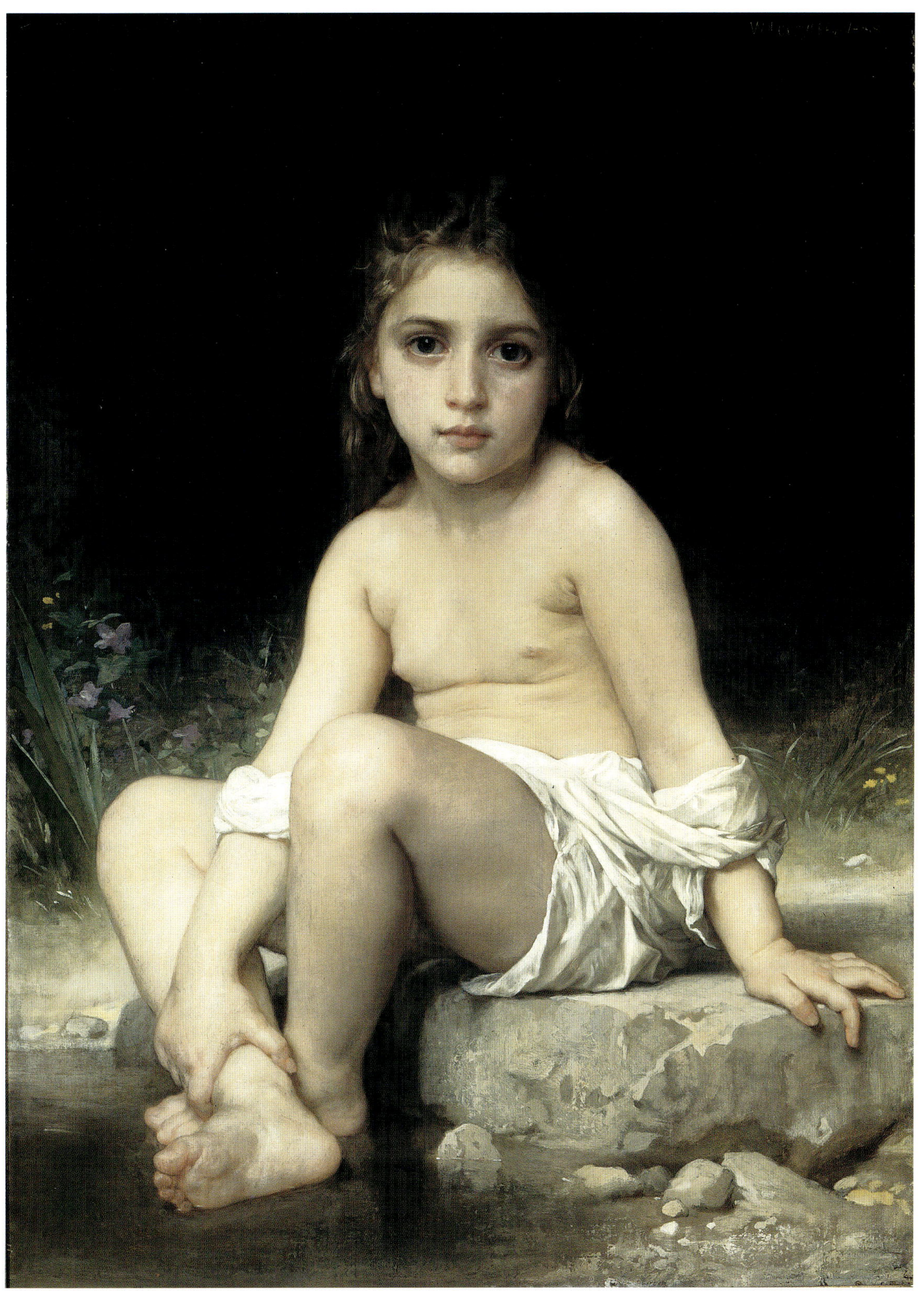

William Adolphe Bouguereau, *Child at Bath (Petite fille assise au bord de l'eau),* 1886 (cat. no. 3)

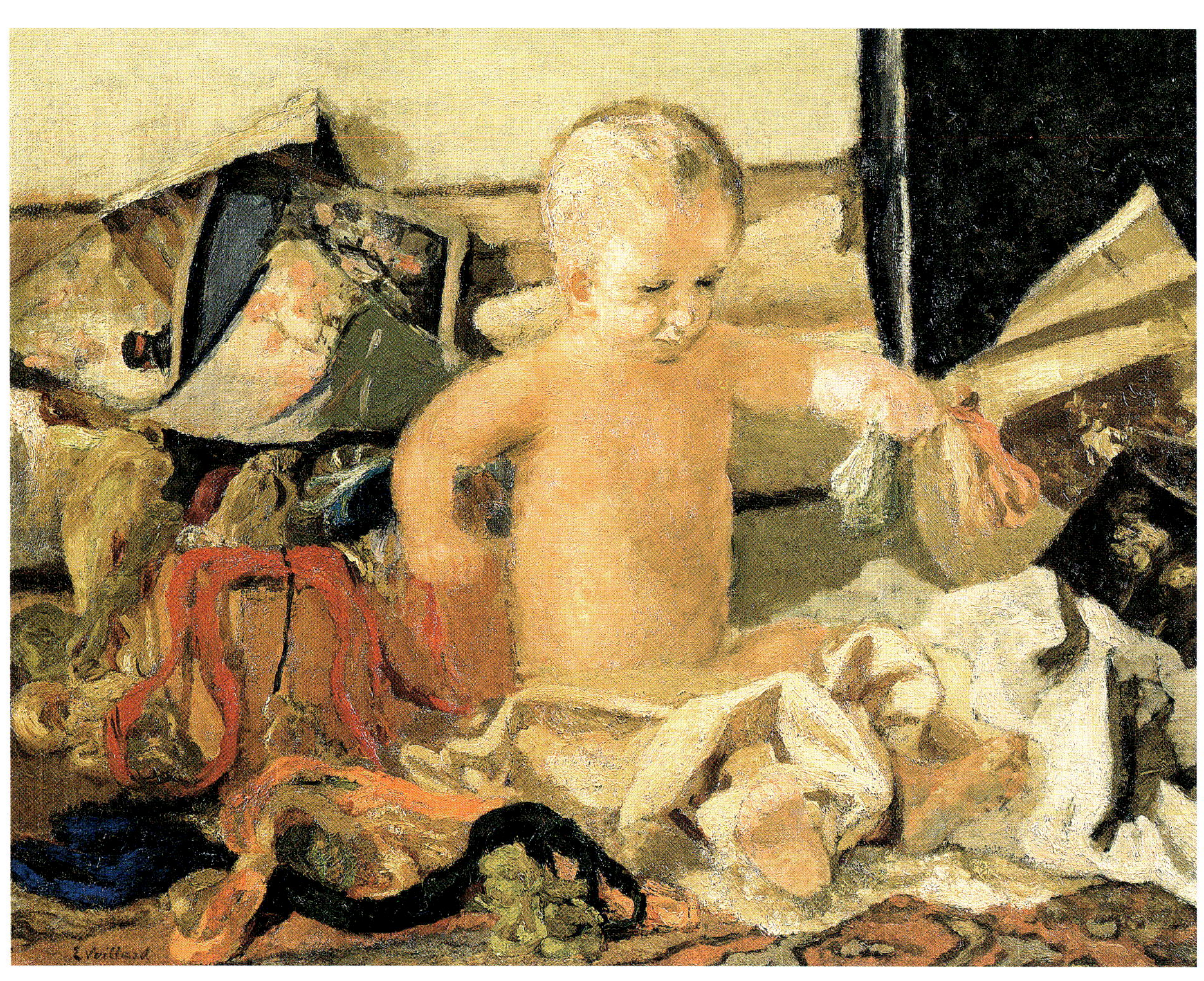

Édouard Vuillard
Child with Ribbons (Enfant aux rubans), c. 1904-05
(cat. no. 55)

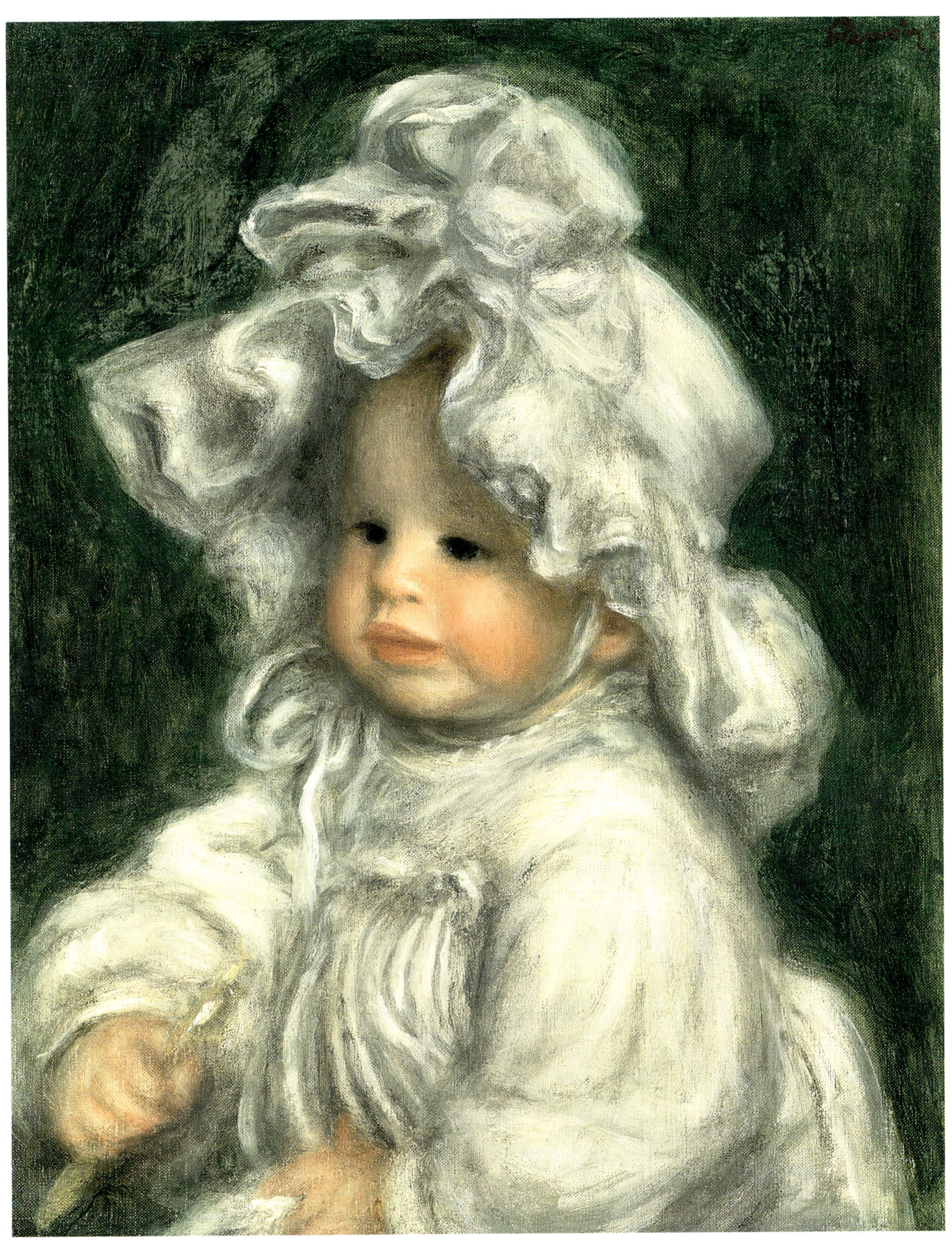

Pierre-Auguste Renoir, *Portrait of Coco,* 1902 (cat. no. 39)

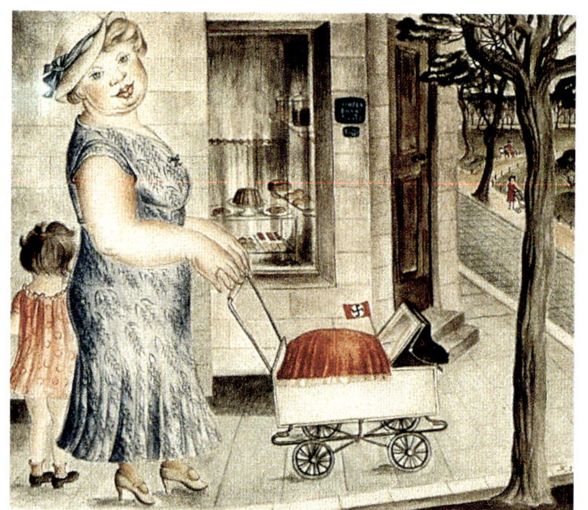

Dorothea Wüsten Koeppen
A Woman of 1934 (Eine Frau von 1934), 1934
(cat. no. 26)

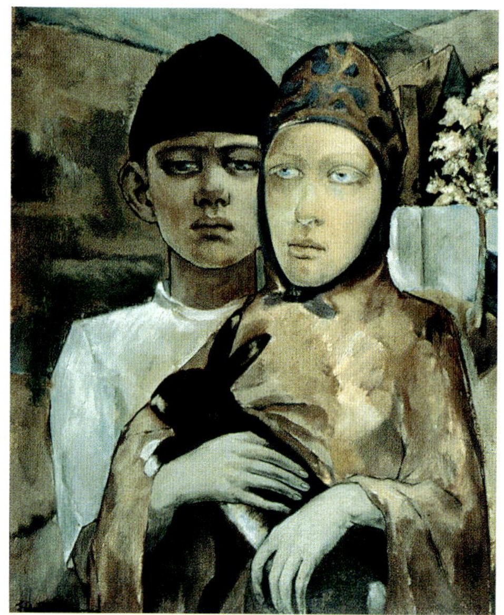

Fritz Burmann
Farmer's Children (Two Children with a Hare)
(Bauernkinder [Zwei Kinder mit Hasen]), 1923
(cat. no. 6)

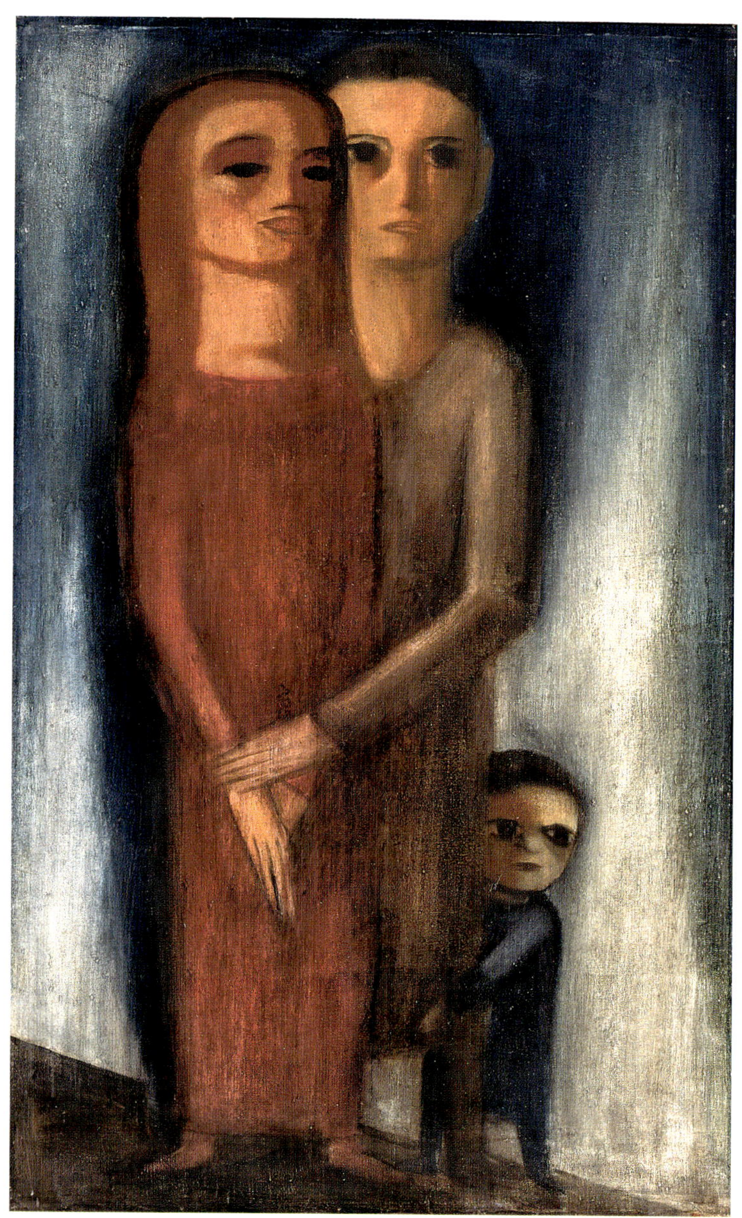

Karl Völker
Gypsy Family, c. 1920
(cat. no. 54)

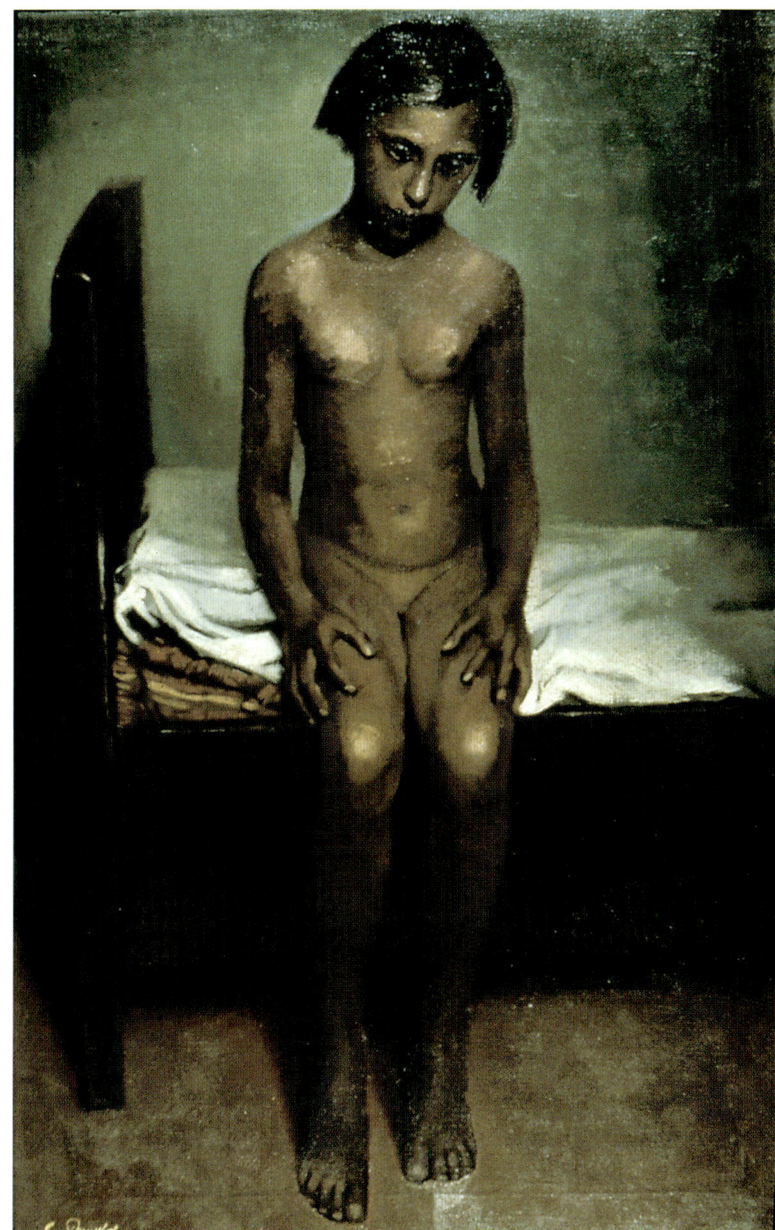

Ernest Neuschul
Nude Girl (Jung-Mädchen Akt), 1930
(cat. no. 35)

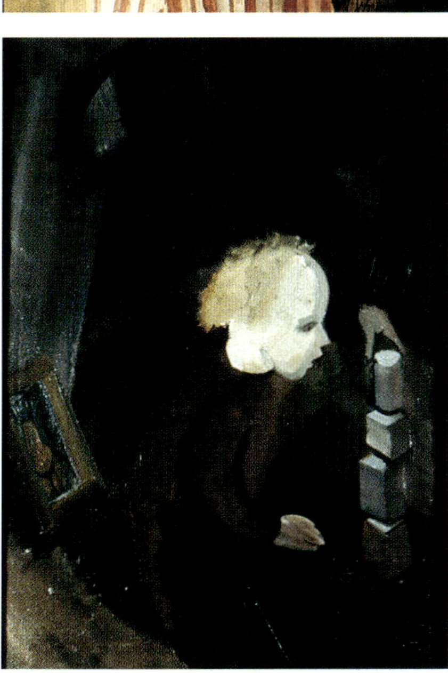

Martel Schwichtenberg
Girl in Red Striped Skirt (Mädchen in rotgestreiftem Kleid), c. 1920?
(cat. no. 43)

Otto Herbig
The Sick Boy (Der kranke Junge), 1923
(cat. no. 21)

Julius Hüther
Pleasures of Winter (Winterfreude), 1931
(cat. no. 23)

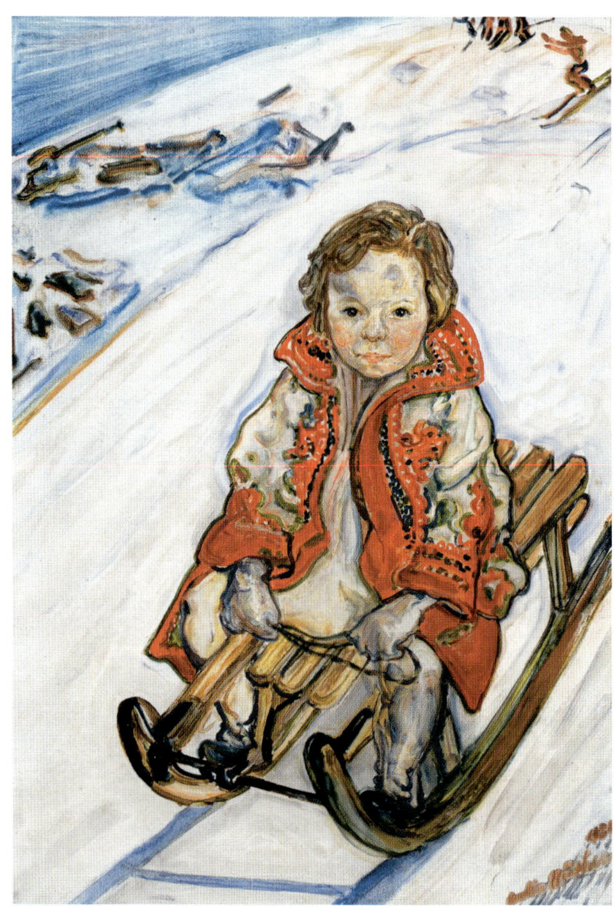

Joaquín Sorolla y Bastida
Drawing in the Sand, c. 1911
(cat. no. 47)

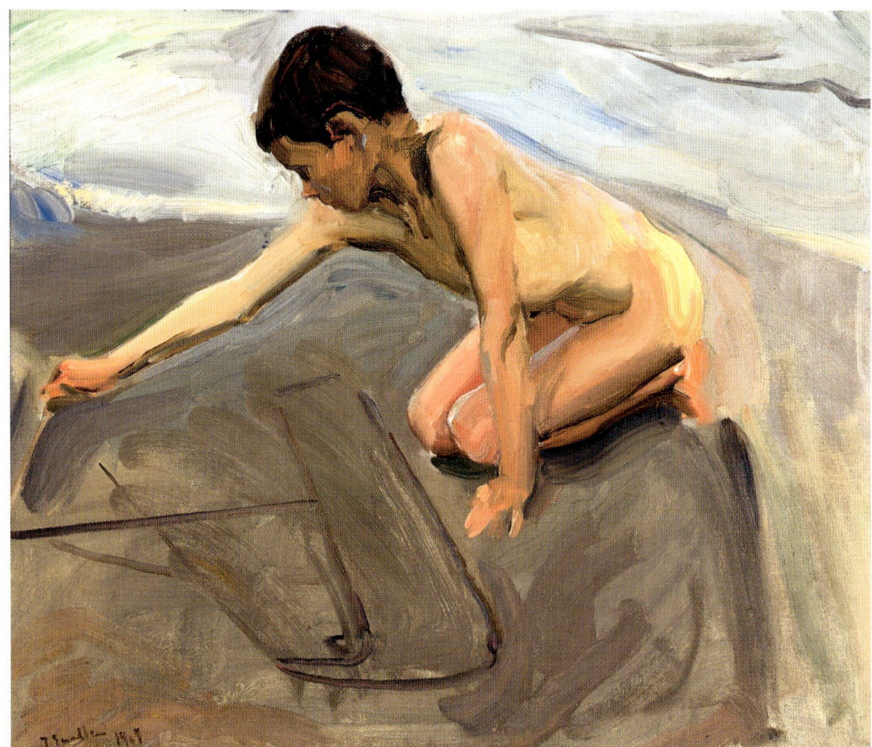

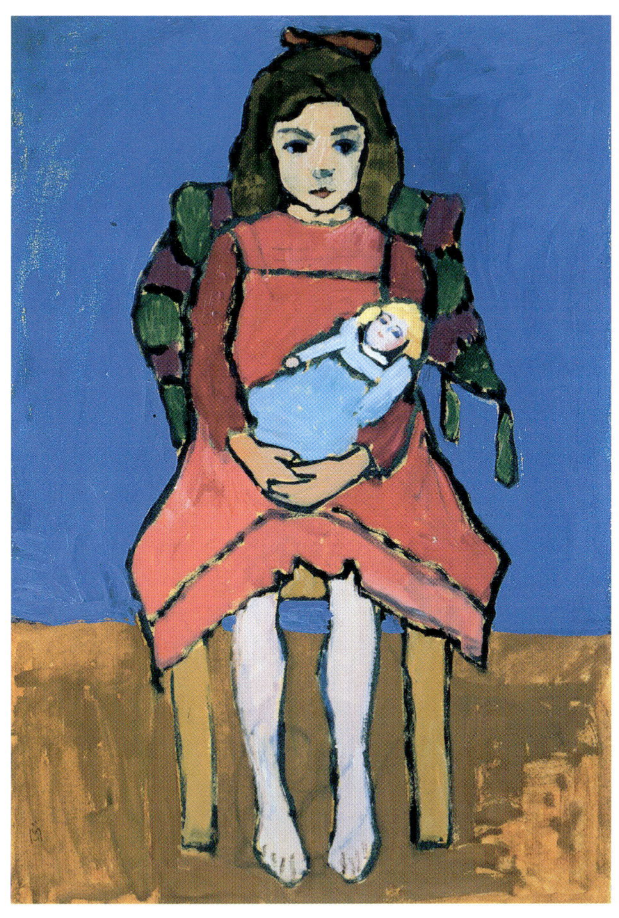

Gabriele Münter
Girl with Doll (Mädchen mit Puppe), 1908-09
(cat. no. 34)

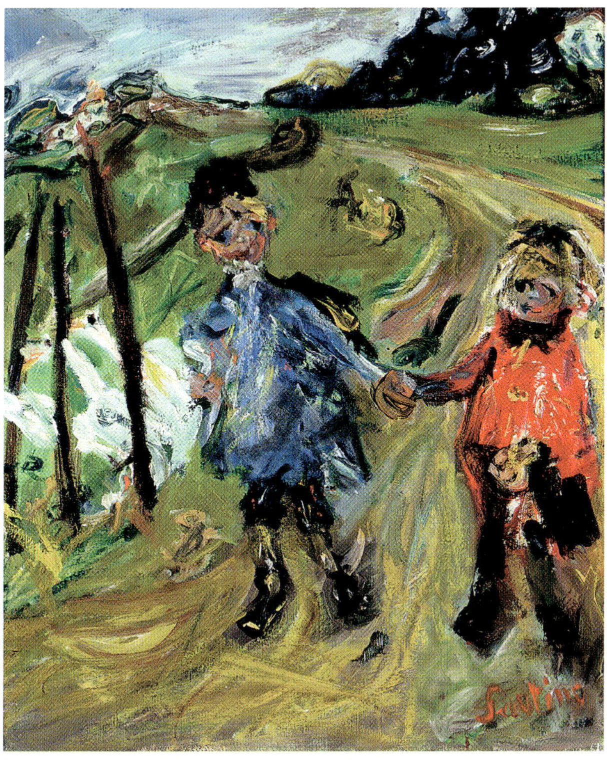

Chaim Soutine
Children and Geese, 1934
(cat. no. 48)

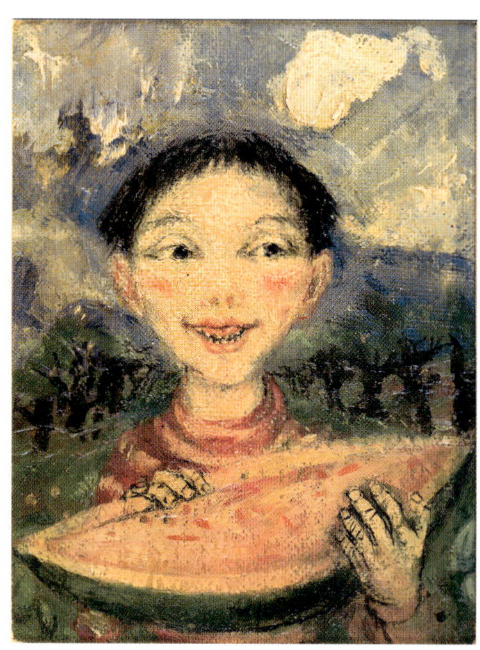

Philip Evergood
Laughing Boy, 1945
(cat. no. 16)

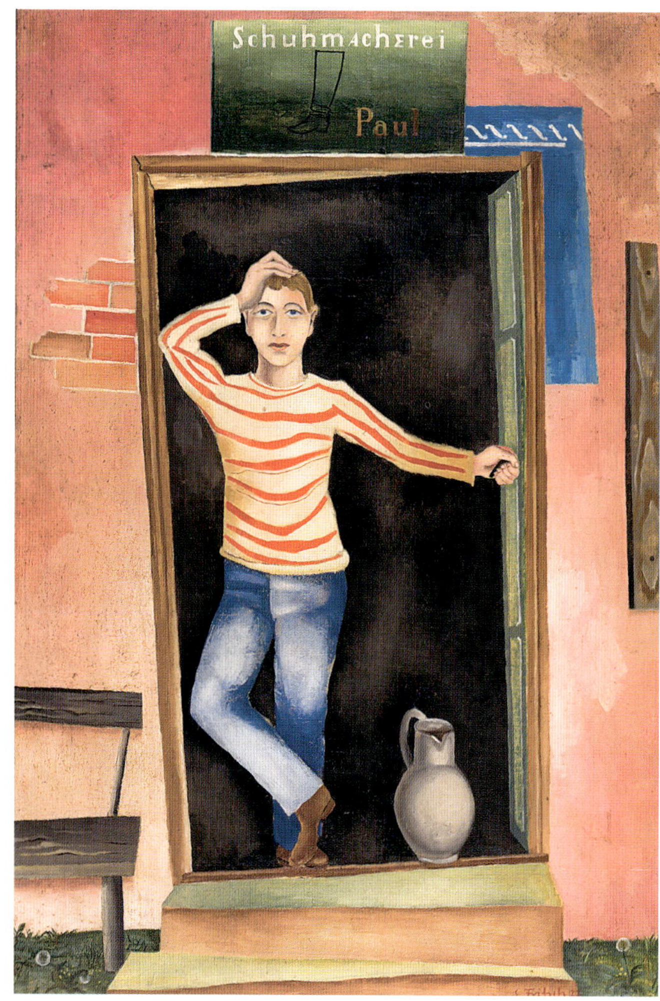

Ernst Fritsch
Son of the Shoemaker
(*Der Sohn des Schumachers*), 1922
(cat. no. 19)

Checklist of the Exhibition

(Height precedes width in dimensions)

1. Milton Avery
American (1885-1965)
Maternity, 1933
Oil on canvas
30 x 25 in.
Collection of David Barnett Gallery, Milwaukee

Provenance: Mrs. Milton Avery
Exhibition: Milwaukee, David Barnett Gallery, *Milton Avery: The 1930's Period,* 14 May-23 July 1988, cat. no. 40, illus. p. 17

2. Edwin Howland Blashfield
American (1848-1936)
Waterloo: Total Defeat, 1882
Oil on canvas
20 x 15 in.
Collection of Edward Wilson,
Fund for Fine Arts, Chevy Chase, Maryland

Provenance: The Arden Collection
Exhibitions: New York, National Academy of Design, 1882, no. 494; Yonkers, New York, Hudson River Museum, *Domestic Bliss,* 1986, cat. no. 45, illus.
Literature: Anita Schorsch, *Images of Childhood: An Illustrated Social History* (New York: Mayflower Books, 1979), illus. p. 98; Elizabeth L. O'Leary, *At Beck and Call: The Representation of Domestic Servants in Nineteenth-Century American Painting* (Washington, D. C.: Smithsonian Institution Press, 1996), illus. plate 7

3. William Adolphe Bouguereau
French (1825-1905)
Child at Bath (Petite fille assise au bord de l'eau), 1886
Oil on canvas
33 x 24 5/16 in.
Henry Art Gallery, University of Washington-Seattle, Horace C. Henry Collection
26.12

Provenance: Sold by the artist, 4 April 1886, Goupil, Paris, no. 17991; sold 8 May 1886; M. Knoedler & Co., New York; General Russel A. Alger; Horace C. Henry, 1923; his gift to the University of Washington, 1926
Literature: Marius Vachon, *W. Bouguereau* (Paris: A. Lahure, 1900), p. 156 (as *Petite fille accroupie*); Joseph N. Newland, ed., *Henry Art Gallery* (Seattle: University of Washington), illus. p. 23; Robert Isaacson, *William-Adolphe Bouguereau* (New York: New York Cultural Center, 1974); Richard Grove, comp., *Henry Art Gallery: Four Decades* (Seattle: Henry Gallery Association, Inc., 1977), illus. p. 75; Fronia E. Wissman, *Bouguereau* (San Francisco: Pomegranate ArtBooks, 1996), illus. p. 63

4. John George Brown
American (1831-1913)
Eating the Profits, 1878
Oil on canvas
21 x 17 in.
Collection of Edward Wilson,
Fund for Fine Arts, Chevy Chase, Maryland

5. John George Brown
American (1831-1913)
The Card Trick, c. 1880s
Oil on canvas
25 x 30 in.
Joslyn Art Museum, Omaha, Nebraska,
Gift of the Estate of Mrs. Sarah Joslyn
JAM 1944.14

Provenance: Mr. George Joslyn, by 1896; gift to Joslyn Art Museum from the estate of Mrs. George (Sarah) Joslyn, 1944
Exhibitions: Chicago Columbia Exposition, 1893; Lincoln, Sheldon Gallery, University of Nebraska, 19 November-16 December 1968; Washington, D. C., The Corcoran Gallery of Art, *Facing History: The Black Image in American Art, 1710-1940,* 13 January-25 March 1990

(traveled to the Brooklyn Museum of Art), illus. p. 95; Omaha, Joslyn Art Museum, *Worth a Thousand Words: Nineteenth-Century Academic Paintings,* 20 January-20 March 1994
Literature: Ripley Hitchcock, *The Art of the World,* 1895; *The Washington Post,* "Black Images in American Art," 14 January 1990, illus.; Ann Alexander, *Virginia Cavalcade,* winter 1991, p. 128, illus. only; Kathleen Pacidi, "Beyond Bootblacks: *The Boat Builder* and the Art of John George Brown," *The Bulletin of the Cleveland Museum of Art,* January 1991; *Revisiting the White City: American Art at the 1893 World's Fair,* exh. cat. (Washington, D. C.: National Museum of American Art, 1993), illus. p. 213, no. 536

6. Fritz Burmann
German (1892-1945)
Farmer's Children (Two Children with a Hare) (Bauernkinder [Zwei Kinder mit Hasen]), 1923
Oil on canvas
20 15/16 x 17 1/2 in.
Collection of Marvin and Janet Fishman, Milwaukee

Provenance: Private collection, Germany; Kunsthaus Lempertz, Cologne
Exhibitions: Milwaukee, UWM Art Museum, University of Wisconsin, *Reactions to the War: European Art, 1914-1925,* 2 November-14 December 1986, cat. no. 6; Milwaukee Art Museum, *From Expressionism to Resistance: Art in Germany 1909-1936—The Marvin and Janet Fishman Collection,* 6 December 1990-3 February 1991 (traveled to Berlin, Berlinische Galerie; Frankfurt, Schirn Kunsthalle; Emden, Kunsthalle Emden; New York, The Jewish Museum; Omaha, Joslyn Art Museum; and Atlanta, High Museum), cat. no. 22, illus. p. 37; Stockholm, Liljevalchs Konsthall, *Konst Som Motstånd: Samling Marving och Janet Fishman,* 18 November 1995-7 January 1996 (traveled to The Hague, Geementemuseum and Paleis Lange Voorhout; Helsinki, Helsingen Taidehalli; and Brussels, Palais de Beaux-Arts), cat. no. 17

7. Thomas Mickell Burnham
American (1818-1866)
The Young Artist, 1840
Oil on canvas
25 x 30 in.
Collection of Hirschl and Adler Galleries, New York

Provenance: The artist; to sale, Apollo Association, New York, 1843; A. P. Kimball, Boston, Mass.; The Boston Athenaeum, by 1846 until about 1910-20
Exhibitions: Mass., The Boston Athenaeum, 1840, no. 31; New York: Apollo Association, 1841, no. 108; Apollo Association, 1843, no. 17; The Boston Athenaeum, 1846, no. 127; 1847, no. 131; 1848, no. 6; 1850, no. 175; 1852, no. 70; 1853, no. 51; 1855, no. 7; 1856, no. 57; 1857, no. 16; 1859, nos. 123 and 124; 1860, no. 107 and in 2nd edition, no. 120; 1861, no. 86; 1862, no. 86; 1863, no. 55; 1864, no. 69; 1865, no. 68; 1866, no. 68; 1867, no. 71; 1868, no. 71; 1869, no. 71; 1870, no. 245; 1872, no. 220

8. Mary Cassatt
American (1844-1926)
Peasant Mother and Child, c. 1894
Aquatint and drypoint with monotype printing and hand coloring
11 11/16 x 9 5/16 in.
Collection of Dr. and Mrs. Robert S. Pavlic, Brookfield

Literature: Nancy Mowll Mathews and Barbara Stern Shapiro, *Mary Cassatt: The Color Prints,* exh. cat. (Williamstown, Mass.: Williams College Museum of Art, 1989), no. 17, pp. 168-73, 170, illus. (another version)

9. Mary Cassatt
American (1844-1926)
Baby John Asleep, Sucking His Thumb, c. 1910
Pastel on paper
26 x 21 7/8 in.
Collection of Catherine and David A. Straz, Jr., Milwaukee

Provenance: Sold, Galerie Georges Petit, Paris, vente Frederic Mallet, 20-22 May 1920, lot 16; Francisco Llobet, Buenos Aires; his daughter, Ernestina Llobet Llavallol, Buenos Aires; Richard Pfeil, Naples, Fla.; sold, Sotheby's, New York, 12 November 1996, lot 3, illus.
Exhibitions: Buenos Aires, Museo Nacional de Bellas Artes, *El impresionismo frances en las colecciones argentinas,* 1962, no. 16; Georgia, The Columbus Museum of Art (and traveling), *Masterworks of American Impressionism,* 1992-94, no. 18
Literature: Adelyn Dohme Breeskin, *Mary Cassatt, A Catalogue Raisonné of the Oils, Pastels, Watercolors and Drawings* (Washington, D. C., 1970), no. 578, illus. p. 208

10. Marc Chagall
Russian (1887-1985)
Grey Village
Lithograph
26 1/2 x 20 1/8 in.
Collection of Dr. and Mrs. Milton F. Gutglass, Milwaukee

11. Eyre Crowe
English (1824-1910)
Boys of Blue Coat School, 1877
Oil on board
7 1/8 x 9 3/4 in.
Collection of Edward Wilson,
Fund for Fine Arts, Chevy Chase, Maryland

12. Alfred De Dreux
French (1810-1860)
Innocence between Two Thieves
(L'Innocence entre deux larrons), c. 1859
Oil on canvas
55 1/8 x 67 7/8 in.
Private Collection

Provenance: Baron de Croze; Madame Paul Hottinguer, née Christine Robinet de Plas, Domaine de Champ-Brûlé, Fontenailles
Exhibition: Paris, Galerie La Cymaise, *Alfred de Dreux,* 20 September-29 October 1988, illus. p. 21
Literature: Forthcoming catalogue raisonné of the works of Alfred De Dreux by M.-C. Renauld-Beaupère, P. Brame, and B. Lorenceau

13. Franz von Defregger
Austrian (1835-1921)
The Story Teller, 1870
Oil on canvas
16 x 19 1/2 in.
Milwaukee Art Museum, Gift of the
René von Schleinitz Foundation, M1962.38

Literature: For documentation see Rudolf M. Bisanz, *The René von Schleinitz Collection of the Milwaukee Art Center: Major Schools of German Nineteenth-Century Painting* (Milwaukee and Madison: Milwaukee Art Center and The University of Wisconsin Press, 1980), no. 18, p. 67, illus.

14. Otto Dix
German (1891-1969)
Sunday Outing (Sonntagsspaziergang), 1922
Oil and tempera on canvas
29 1/2 x 23 5/8 in.
Collection of Marvin and Janet Fishman,
Milwaukee

Provenance: *Neue Kunst,* Frau Ey, Düsseldorf; Dr. Hans Koch, Düsseldorf; Adalbert Trillhaase, Düsseldorf; Hans Joachim Ziersch, Switzerland
Exhibitions: Munich, Museum Villa Stuck, *Otto Dix 1891-1969,* 23 August-27 October, 1987, cat. no. 190;

Marc Chagall, *Grey Village* (cat. no. 10)

Milwaukee Art Museum, *From Expressionism to Resistance: Art in Germany 1909-1936—The Marvin and Janet Fishman Collection,* 6 December 1990-3 February 1991 (traveled to Berlin, Berlinische Galerie; Frankfurt, Schirn Kunsthalle; Emden, Kunsthalle Emden; New York, The Jewish Museum; Omaha, Joslyn Art Museum; and Atlanta, High Museum), cat. no. 28, illus. p. 43; Stockholm, Liljevalchs Konsthall, *Konst Som Motstånd: Samling Marving och Janet Fishman,* 18 November 1995-7 January 1996 (traveled to The Hague, Geementemuseum and Paleis Lange Voorhout; Helsinki, Helsingen Taidehalli; and Brussels, Palais de Beaux-Arts), cat. no. 27, illus. p. 65

15. Otto Dix
German (1891-1969)
Workers' Children (Arbeiterkinder), 1922
Pen and ink, watercolor on Japan paper
20 5/8 x 14 11/16 in.
Collection of Marvin and Janet Fishman,
Milwaukee

Provenance: Private collection, New York; Alien Custodian Property Auction, New York, 1952

Exhibitions: Milwaukee, UWM Art Museum, University of Wisconsin, *Reactions to the War: European Art, 1914-1925*, 2 November-14 December 1986, cat. no. 14; Milwaukee Art Museum, *From Expressionism to Resistance: Art in Germany 1909-1936—The Marvin and Janet Fishman Collection*, 6 December 1990-3 February 1991 (traveled to Berlin, Berlinische Galerie; Frankfurt, Schirn Kunsthalle; Emden, Kunsthalle Emden; New York, The Jewish Museum; Omaha, Joslyn Art Museum; and Atlanta, High Museum), cat. no. 26, illus. p. 40; Stockholm, Liljevalchs Konsthall, *Konst Som Motstånd: Samling Marving och Janet Fishman*, 18 November 1995-7 January 1996 (traveled to The Hague, Geementemuseum and Paleis Lange Voorhout; Helsinki, Helsingen Taidehalli; and Brussels, Palais de Beaux-Arts), cat. no. 23, illus. p. 61; Milwaukee, Patrick and Beatrice Haggerty Museum of Art, Marquette University, *Rudolf Schlichter and Friends: German Art between the Wars*, 26 June-31 August 1997

16. Philip Evergood
American (1901-1973)
Laughing Boy, 1945
Oil on board
10 5/16 x 8 in.
Collection of Jean Carter, Milwaukee

Provenance: Collection of the artist; Frank Kleinholz

17. Pierre Édouard Frère
French (1819-1886)
Young Admiral (Le jeune admiral), c. 1860
Oil on paper mounted on canvas
12 1/2 x 9 1/2 in.
Collection of Edward Wilson,
Fund for Fine Arts, Chevy Chase, Maryland

18. Pierre Édouard Frère
French (1819-1886)
Playing Mother (Jouant maman), 1865
Oil on panel
9 3/4 x 7 3/4 in.
Collection of Edward Wilson,
Fund for Fine Arts, Chevy Chase, Maryland

19. Ernst Fritsch
German (1892-1962)
Son of the Shoemaker (Der Sohn des Schumachers), 1922
Oil on canvas
45 7/8 x 31 1/8 in.
Collection of Kevin and Margaret Kinney,
Milwaukee

Provenance: Else Fritsch (widow of the artist), 1972
Exhibition: Berlin, Akademie der Künste, *Rückblick und Gegenwart*, 1963, cat. no. 62
Literature: Wieland Schmied, *Neue Sachlichkeit und Magischer Realismus in Deutschland 1918-1933* (Hannover: Fackelträger Verlag, 1969); Helga Kleimann, *Die Novembergruppe* (Berlin: Gebr. Mann Verlag, 1969); Peter Junk and Wendelin Zimmer, *Felix Nussbaum, Leben und Werk* (Cologne: DuMont Buchverlag, and Bramsche, Rasch Verlag, 1982)

20. Norbert Goeneutte
French (1854-1894)
Reine Goeneutte Washing the Young Jean Geurard in the Artist's Studio, 1889
Oil on canvas
57 x 45 1/4 in.
Collection of Schiller and Bodo European Paintings, New York

Exhibitions: Paris, Salon of 1889, no. 1186; Paris, École des Beaux Arts, *Retrospective Norbert Goeneutte*, 20-30 April 1895, no. 18
Literature: Gilbert de Knyff, *Norbert Goeneutte, sa vie, son oeuvre* (Paris: Mayer Edition, 1978), pp. 99-102, illus. p. 101; forthcoming *Goeneutte Catalogue Raisonné* by Norbert-Georges Goeneutte

21. Otto Herbig
German (1889-1971)
The Sick Boy (Der kranke Junge), 1923
Oil on canvas
29 3/8 x 22 1/16 in.
Collection of Marvin and Janet Fishman, Milwaukee

Provenance: Galerie Ferdinand Möller, Berlin; Wilhelm Valentiner, Berlin and Detroit; Brigid Valentiner-Bertoia, Barto, Pa.; Olympia Gallery, Philadelphia
Exhibitions: Berlin, *Juriefreie Kunstschau*, 1924, cat. no. 513; Milwaukee Art Museum, *From Expressionism to Resistance: Art in Germany 1909-1936—The Marvin and Janet Fishman Collection*, 6 December 1990-3 February 1991 (traveled to Berlin, Berlinische Galerie; Frankfurt, Schirn Kunsthalle; Emden, Kunsthalle Emden; New York, The Jewish Museum; Omaha, Joslyn Art Museum; and Atlanta, High Museum), cat. no. 62, illus. p. 67 (as *The Tower*); Stockholm, Liljevalchs Konsthall, *Konst Som Motstånd: Samling Marving och Janet Fishman*, 18 November 1995-7 January 1996 (traveled to The Hague, Geementemuseum and Paleis Lange Voorhout; Helsinki, Helsingen Taidehalli; and Brussels, Palais de Beaux-Arts), cat. no. 63, illus. p. 87

22. Karl Holtz
German (1899-1978)
Farmer's Child (Bauernjunge), c. 1921
Pencil on paper
11 1/4 x 7 13/16 in.
Collection of Marvin and Janet Fishman, Milwaukee

Provenance: Estate of the artist; Galerie Bodo Niemann, Berlin; Galerie Michael Hasenclever, Munich
Exhibitions: Milwaukee Art Museum, *From Expressionism to Resistance: Art in Germany 1909-1936—The Marvin and Janet Fishman Collection,* 6 December 1990-3 February 1991 (traveled to Berlin, Berlinische Galerie; Frankfurt, Schirn Kunsthalle; Emden, Kunsthalle Emden; New York, The Jewish Museum; Omaha, Joslyn Art Museum; and Atlanta, High Museum), cat. no. 66, illus. p. 69; Stockholm, Liljevalchs Konsthall, *Konst Som Motstånd: Samling Marving och Janet Fishman,* 18 November 1995-7 January 1996 (traveled to The Hague, Geementemuseum and Paleis Lange Voorhout; Helsinki, Helsingen Taidehalli; and Brussels, Palais de Beaux-Arts), cat. no. 66

23. Julius Hüther
German (1881-1954)
Pleasures of Winter (Winterfreude), 1931
Oil on canvas
39 1/2 x 27 1/2 in.
Haggerty Museum of Art,
Gift of Marvin and Janet Fishman
87.4.1

Literature: *Selected Works* (Milwaukee: Patrick and Beatrice Haggerty Museum of Art, Marquette University, 1984), illus. p. 161

24. Jozef Israëls
Dutch (1824-1911)
Dutch Interior (called *Mother and Child*), c. 1898
Oil on canvas
38 1/4 x 52 in.
Haggerty Museum of Art,
Gift of Mr. I. A. Dinerstein
59.13

Provenance: Apparently in the collection of Van Nievelt, The Hague, 1904; Mr. I. A. Dinerstein; his gift to Marquette University, 1959
Literature: Jan Veth, *Josef Israels und seine Kunst* (1906; reprint, The Hague, 1910), p. 15, plate 2; *Selected Works* (Milwaukee: Patrick and Beatrice Haggerty Museum of Art, Marquette University, 1984), pp. 62-63, illus. p. 63

25. William Sergeant Kendall
American (1869-1938)
A Statuette, 1915
Oil on canvas
54 1/4 x 42 3/8 in.
Lent by the Brooklyn Museum of Art,
Gift of Mrs. William Sergeant Kendall, 45.165

26. Dorothea Wüsten Koeppen
German (1893-1967)
A Woman of 1934 (Eine Frau von 1934), 1934
Watercolor over pencil, pen and ink on paper
10 x 11 3/4 in.
Collection of Marvin and Janet Fishman, Milwaukee

Exhibitions: Munich, Galerie Michael Hasenclever, *Aquarelle und Zeichnungen der Zwanziger Jahre,* 1 March-4 April 1987, cat. no. 52; Milwaukee Art Museum, *From Expressionism to Resistance: Art in Germany 1909-1936—The Marvin and Janet Fishman Collection,* 6 December 1990-3 February 1991 (traveled to Berlin, Berlinische Galerie; Frankfurt, Schirn Kunsthalle; Emden, Kunsthalle Emden; New York, The Jewish Museum; Omaha, Joslyn Art Museum; and Atlanta, High Museum), cat. no. 82, illus. p. 82; Stockholm, Liljevalchs Konsthall, *Konst Som Motstånd: Samling Marving och Janet Fishman,* 18 November 1995-7 January 1996 (traveled to The Hague, Geementemuseum and Paleis Lange Voorhout; Helsinki, Helsingen Taidehalli; and Brussels, Palais de Beaux-Arts), cat. no. 83, illus. p. 102

27. Bernhard Kretzschmar
German (1889-1972)
Standing Boy (Stehender Knabe), 1921
Pencil on paper
14 1/2 x 12 1/8 in.
Collection of Marvin and Janet Fishman, Milwaukee

Exhibitions: Munich, Galerie Michael Hasenclever, *Überblick: Zehn Jahre Galerie Michael Hasenclever,* 1982; Milwaukee Art Museum, *From Expressionism to Resistance: Art in Germany 1909-1936—The Marvin and Janet Fishman Collection,* 6 December 1990-3 February 1991 (traveled to Berlin, Berlinische Galerie; Frankfurt, Schirn Kunsthalle; Emden, Kunsthalle Emden; New York, The Jewish Museum; Omaha, Joslyn Art Museum; and Atlanta, High Museum), cat. no. 83, illus. p. 83; Stockholm, Liljevalchs Konsthall, *Konst Som Motstånd: Samling Marving och Janet Fishman,* 18 November 1995-7 January 1996 (traveled to The Hague, Geementemuseum and Paleis Lange Voorhout; Helsinki, Helsingen Taidehalli; and Brussels, Palais de Beaux-Arts), cat. no. 84, illus. p. 103

28. Wilhelm Lachnit
German (1899-1962)
Boy in Sailor Suit (Knabe in Matrosenjacke), 1923
Carpenter's pencil on paper
18 1/8 x 13 1/8 in.
Collection of Marvin and Janet Fishman, Milwaukee

Provenance: Collection Peter Hielscher, Dresden; private collection, Germany; Galerie Bodo Niemann, Berlin; Galerie Michael Hasenclever, Munich
Exhibitions: West Berlin, Neue Gesellschaft für Bildende Kunst, *Wem gehört die Welt: Kunst und Gesellschaft in der Weimarer Republik*, 1977 (traveled to Stockholm, Moderna Museet, 1978), cat. no. 345; Munich, Galerie Michael Hasenclever, *Aquarelle und Zeichnungen der Zwanziger Jahre*, 1 March-4 April 1987, cat. no. 55 (as *Arbeiterjunge*); Milwaukee Art Museum, *From Expressionism to Resistance: Art in Germany 1909-1936—The Marvin and Janet Fishman Collection*, 6 December 1990-3 February 1991 (traveled to Berlin, Berlinische Galerie; Frankfurt, Schirn Kunsthalle; Emden, Kunsthalle Emden; New York, The Jewish Museum; Omaha, Joslyn Art Museum; and Atlanta, High Museum), cat. no. 84, illus. p. 83; Stockholm, Liljevalchs Konsthall, *Konst Som Motstånd: Samling Marving och Janet Fishman*, 18 November 1995-7 January 1996 (traveled to The Hague, Geementemuseum and Paleis Lange Voorhout; Helsinki, Helsingen Taidehalli; and Brussels, Palais de Beaux-Arts), cat. no. 85, illus. p. 104

29. Jacob Lawrence
American (b. 1917)
Birth, 1948
Tempera on board
20 x 16 in.
Haggerty Museum of Art, Museum Purchase, The Mary B. Finnigan Art Endowment Fund 94.18

Provenance: Collection of the artist; Pinellas Family Collection; Mr. Joel Corcos Levy, New York; Michael Rosenfeld Gallery, New York; Haggerty Museum of Art purchase, 1994
Exhibitions: New York, Michael Rosenfeld Gallery, *African-American Art: Twentieth-Century Masterworks*, November 1993-February 1994, p. 13; Milwaukee Art Museum, *Collectively Speaking: African-American Art from Area Collections*, 1 March-28 April 1996; Seattle, Henry Art Gallery, University of Washington, *Jacob Lawrence: Painting Life*, 2 July-27 September 1998
Literature: Forthcoming catalogue raisonné by the Jacob Lawrence Catalogue Raisonné Project, Seattle and on-line catalogue in conjunction with the University of Washington Digital Library Initiatives and Center for Information Systems Optimization (http://content.lib.washington.edu/Jacob/index.html)

30. Max Liebermann
German (1847-1935)
The Cobbler's Girl, 1871
Oil on canvas
41 x 26 in.
Private Collection

Provenance: Sold by the artist, 1871; Galerie Rudolph Lepke, Berlin; Joseph Stern, Berlin, as of 1906; Galerie Thannhauser, Munich, by 1918; Mairowsky collection, Berlin and Geneva
Exhibitions: Berlin, Königliche Nationalgalerie, *Ausstellung deutscher Kunst aus der Zeit von 1775-1875*, 1906, II, no. 1064, illus, p. 349; Berlin, Königliche Akademie der Künste, *Max Liebermann—Ausstellung zum 70. Geburstage des Künstlers*, July-August 1917, no. 3; Berlin, Moderne Galerie Thannhauser, *Eröffnungsausstellung*, 1927, no. 156, illus. p. 67; St. Gallen, Kunstmuseum, *Max Liebermann 1847-1935*, 28 August-31 October 1948, no. 1, illus.; Berlin, Staatliche Museen, Preussischer Kulturbesitz, Nationalgalerie, *Max Liebermann in seiner Zeit*, 6 September-4 November 1979 (traveled to Munich, Haus de Kunst), no. 4, illus.; The Hague, Gemeentemuseum, *Max Liebermann en Holland*, 21 March-26 May 1980, no. 2, illus. p. 43
Literature: C. Langhammer, "Die Entwicklung Max Liebermanns," *Deutsche Junst* II (3), 2 November 1897, illus. p. 11; H. Rosenhagen, "Max Liebermann," *Velhagen & Klasings Monatshefte* XXI (11), July 1907, illus. p. 498; G. Pauli, *Max Liebermann, des Meisters Gemälde* (Stuttgart and Leipzig, 1911), illus. p. 5 (1921 ed., illus. pl. 2); K. Scheffler, *Max Liebermann* (Munich, 1912), p. 126 (1922 ed., p. 112); E. Hancke, *Max Liebermann, sein Leben und seine Werke* (Berlin, 1914), pp. 62, 101, 528; Galerie Tannhauser, *Nachtragswerk III zur grossen Katalog-Ausgabe 1916* (Munich, 1918), illus. pl. 99; E. Hancke, *Max Liebermann, sein Leben und seine Werke* (Berlin, 1923), pp. 62-64; M. J. Friedländer, *Max Liebermann* (Berlin, n.d. [1924]), p. 207, no. 4, illus. p. 25; E. Waldmann, "Max Liebermann zum 80. Geburstag am 20. Juni," *Der Kunstwanderer*, July 1927, illus. p. 445; H. Ostwald, *Das Liebermann-Buch* (Berlin, 1930), p. 108; K. Boskamp, *Studien zum Frühwerk von Max Liebermann mit einem Verzeichnis der Gemälde und Olstudien von 1866-1889* (Hildesheim, Zurich, and New York, 1994), cat. no. 14; M. Eberle, *Liebermann: Werkverzeichnis der Gemälde und Olstudien, 1865-1899* (Munich, 1995), I, pp. 36-37, no. 1871/2, illus. p. 35

31. Nicolas Maes
Dutch (1634-1693)
Mythological Subject, 1673
Oil on canvas
74 x 55 in.
Collection of the Rojtman Foundation,
Courtesy of Lillian Rojtman Berkman

Provenance: Rothschild and Co., London, 1943; B. Rapp, Stockholm, 1950, no. 1057
Literature: *Connoisseur,* November 1962 (cover); Rose Wishnevsky, *Studien zur Portrait Historie in den Niederlanden,* Muenchener Dissertation 67, no. 88; Franklin W. Robinson, *Dutch Life in the Golden Century,* exh. cat. (St. Petersburg, Fla. and Atlanta, Ga.: Museum of Fine Arts and High Museum of Art, 1975)

32. Johann Georg Meyer, called Meyer von Bremen
German (1813-1886)
Girl with Knitting (Ein strickendes Mädchen), 1846
Oil on paper mounted on cardboard
7 x 5 3/8 in.
Milwaukee Art Museum, Gift of the
René von Schleinitz Foundation, M1962.99

Provenance: Galerie Commeter, Hamburg
Literature: For documentation see Rudolf M. Bisanz, *The René von Schleinitz Collection of the Milwaukee Art Center: Major Schools of German Nineteenth-Century Popular Painting* (Milwaukee and Madison: Milwaukee Art Center and The University of Wisconsin Press, 1980), no. 121, p. 177-78, illus.

33. Berthe Morisot
French (1841-1895)
Julie Listening (Julie écoutant), 1888
Oil on canvas
24 1/2 x 18 1/2 in.
Collection of Catherine and David A. Straz, Jr.,
Milwaukee

Provenance: Estate of the artist; Schoneman Gallery, New York; Mr. and Mrs. Richard J. Bernhard, New York: The Bernhard Foundation, Inc., New York; sold, Sotheby Parke Bernet, Inc., New York, 26 May 1976, lot 18; anonymous; sold, Christie's, New York, 12 November 1997, lot 227, illus.
Literature: M. L. Bataille and G. Wildenstein, *Berthe Morisot, Catalogue des peintures, pastels et aquarelles* (Paris, 1961), no. 229, illus. fig. 231; forthcoming revised edition of Morisot catalogue raisonné, vol. 1, *Oil Paintings,* by Yves Rouart, Delphine Montalant, and Alain Clairet

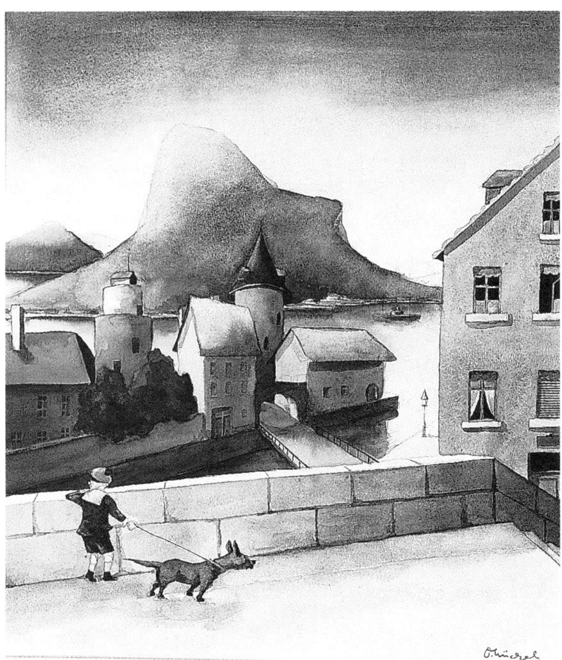

Otto Nückel, *Little Dog Walker,* c. 1924-25
(cat. no. 36)

34. Gabriele Münter
German (1877-1962)
Girl with Doll (Mädchen mit Puppe), 1908-09
Oil on cardboard
27 1/2 x 19 in.
Milwaukee Art Museum, Gift of
Mrs. Harry Lynde Bradley, M1966.165

Provenance: Dalzell Hatfield Galleries, Los Angeles (purchased from the artist); sold, 1963
Exhibitions: Los Angeles, Dalzell Hatfield Galleries, *Gabriele Münter Memorial Exhibition,* 1-25 May 1963; Milwaukee Art Center, *Wisconsin Collects,* 24 September-26 October 1964; Milwaukee Art Center, *The Collection of Mrs. Harry Lynde Bradley,* 25 October 1968-23 February 1969, cat. no. 358, illus. p. 156; Cambridge, Mass., Busch-Reisinger Museum, Harvard University, *Gabriele Münter: Between Munich and Murnau,* 25 September-8 November 1980 (traveled to Princeton University Art Museum), cat. no. 31, illus. p. 35; Lenbachhaus, Städtische Galerie im Lenbachhaus, *Gabriele Münter, 1877-1962,* 27 July-18 October 1992 (traveled to Frankfurt, Schirn Kunsthalle; Stockholm, Liljevalchs Konsthall; and Berlin, Staatliche Kunsthalle), cat. no. 50, p. 262, illus.; Milwaukee Art Museum, *Gabriele Münter: The Years of Expressionism, 1903-1920,* 5 December 1997-1 March 1998 (traveled to Georgia, Columbus

Museum of Art; Richmond, Virginia Museum of Fine Arts; and San Antonio, Marion Koogler McNay Art Museum), cat. no. 28, p. 118, illus. p. 113
Literature: Donald E. Gordon, *Expressionism, Art and Idea* (New Haven, Conn.: Yale University Press, 1987), illus. p. 81, fig. 61

35. Ernest Neuschul
German (1895-1968)
Nude Girl (Jung-Mädchen Akt), 1930
Oil on canvas
29 1/4 x 25 11/16 in.
Collection of Marvin and Janet Fishman, Milwaukee

Provenance: Galerie Nierendorf, West Berlin
Exhibitions: West Berlin, Galerie Nierendorf, *Herbst '84,* 1984; Milwaukee Art Museum, *From Expressionism to Resistance: Art in Germany 1909-1936—The Marvin and Janet Fishman Collection,* 6 December 1990-3 February 1991 (traveled to Berlin, Berlinische Galerie; Frankfurt, Schirn Kunsthalle; Emden, Kunsthalle Emden; New York, The Jewish Museum; Omaha, Joslyn Art Museum; and Atlanta, High Museum), cat. no. 121, illus. p. 111; Stockholm, Liljevalchs Konsthall, *Konst Som Motstånd: Samling Marvin och Janet Fishman,* 18 November 1995-7 January 1996 (traveled to The Hague, Geementemuseum and Paleis Lange Voorhout; Helsinki, Helsingen Taidehalli; and Brussels, Palais de Beaux-Arts), cat. no. 124, illus. p. 127

36. Otto Nückel
German
Little Dog Walker, c. 1924-25
Watercolor on paper
11 1/2 x 10 1/4 in.
Collection of Kevin and Margaret Kinney, Milwaukee

Provenance: Lempertz Auktion Haus

37. John Quinton Pringle
Scottish (1864-1925)
Portrait of a Boy: A Reluctant Subject, 1910
Oil on canvas
21 x 17 in.
Collection of Artemis Fine Arts, Inc., New York

Provenance: The artist, and thence by family descent
Exhibition: Glasglow, Duncan R. Miller Fine Arts, *Aspects of Twentieth Century Scottish Art,* 1996, no. 7, illus.

38. Odilon Redon
French (1840-1916)
Portrait of a Young Boy (Portrait d'un jeune garçon), c. 1906
Pastel on paper
18 1/2 x 10 1/4 in.
Collection of Artemis Fine Arts, Inc., New York

Provenance: Private collection, Switzerland

39. Pierre-Auguste Renoir
French (1841-1919)
Portrait of Coco, 1902
Oil on canvas
16 1/8 x 12 7/8 in.
Private Collection, Switzerland

Provenance: Estate of the artist; Jakob Goldschmidt, New York
Exhibitions: New York, Wildenstein and Co., *Renoir,* 1969, no. 86, illus.; Kunsthall Tübingen, *Auguste Renoir,* 20 January-27 May 1996, illus. p. 283
Literature: Albert André, *L'Atelier de Renoir* (Paris, 1931), vol. 1, illus. no. 270, plate 84

40. Norman Rockwell
American (1894-1978)
The Spelling Bee
Lithograph
13 7/8 x 30 in.
Collection of Dr. and Mrs. Milton F. Gutglass, Milwaukee

41. Walter Dendy Sadler
English (1854-1923)
The Dame's School, c. 1900
Oil on canvas
34 x 26 in.
Joslyn Art Museum, Omaha, Nebraska,
Gift of the Francis S. Gaines Family
JAM 1981.34

Provenance: Charles N. Dietz Collection, c. 1910?, no. 209 in Dietz Collection catalogue (JAM); Francis S. Gaines and Delia Gaines; gift to the Joslyn Art Museum from the Francis S. Gaines Family (Tyler B. Gaines, Frank Gaines and Mary Gaines Martin, children, and Viola F. Gaines, second wife after Delia's demise), 1981
Exhibition: *Angels and Urchins: Images of Children at the Joslyn,* 15 November 1980-1 January 1981, cat. no. 39, fig. 17, p. 41
Literature: Alison Clarke-Stewart, *Child Development* (John Wiley and Sons)

42. Rudolf Schlichter
German (1890-1955)
Circus Children (Zirkuskinder), c. 1924-25?
Pencil on paper
19 9/16 x 16 3/8 in.
Collection of Marvin and Janet Fishman, Milwaukee

Provenance: Hauswedell and Nolte, Hamburg
Exhibitions: Milwaukee Art Museum, *From Expressionism to Resistance: Art in Germany 1909-1936—The Marvin and Janet Fishman Collection*, 6 December 1990-3 February 1991 (traveled to Berlin, Berlinische Galerie; Frankfurt, Schirn Kunsthalle; Emden, Kunsthalle Emden; New York, The Jewish Museum; Omaha, Joslyn Art Museum; and Atlanta, High Museum), cat. no. 137, illus. p. 121; Stockholm, Liljevalchs Konsthall, *Konst Som Motstånd: Samling Marving och Janet Fishman*, 18 November 1995-7 January 1996 (traveled to The Hague, Geementemuseum and Paleis Lange Voorhout; Helsinki, Helsingen Taidehalli; and Brussels, Palais de Beaux-Arts), cat. no. 141, illus. p. 141; Milwaukee, Patrick and Beatrice Haggerty Museum of Art, Marquette University, *Rudolf Schlichter and Friends: German Art between the Wars*, 26 June-31 August 1997

43. Martel Schwichtenberg
German (1896-1945)
Girl in Red Striped Skirt (Mädchen in rotgestreiftem Kleid), c. 1920?
Oil on cardboard
27 7/8 x 19 5/8 in.
Collection of Marvin and Janet Fishman, Milwaukee

Provenance: Galerie Ferdinand Möller, Berlin; Dr. Wilhelm R. Valentiner, Berlin and Detroit; Brigid Valentiner Bertoia, Barto, Pa.; Olympia Gallery, Philadelphia
Exhibition: Milwaukee Art Museum, *From Expressionism to Resistance: Art in Germany 1909-1936—The Marvin and Janet Fishman Collection*, 6 December 1990-3 February 1991 (traveled to Berlin, Berlinische Galerie; Frankfurt, Schirn Kunsthalle; Emden, Kunsthalle Emden; New York, The Jewish Museum; Omaha, Joslyn Art Museum; and Atlanta, High Museum), cat. no. 142, illus. p. 124; Stockholm, Liljevalchs Konsthall, *Konst Som Motstånd: Samling Marving och Janet Fishman*, 18 November 1995-7 January 1996 (traveled to The Hague, Geementemuseum and Paleis Lange Voorhout; Helsinki, Helsingen Taidehalli; and Brussels, Palais de Beaux-Arts), cat. no. 146

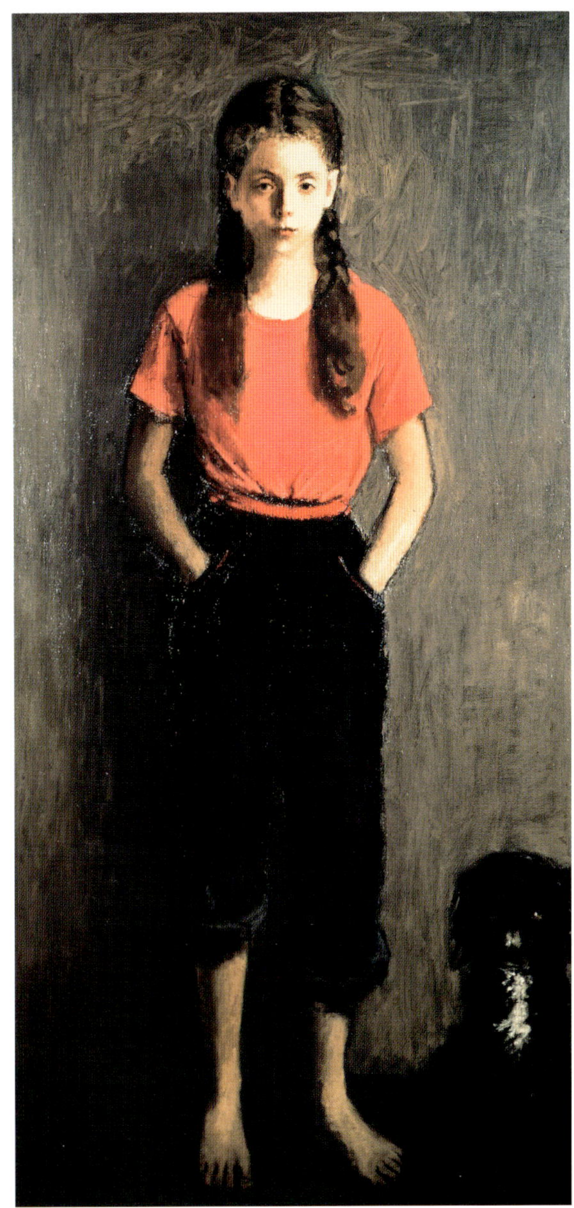

Raphael Soyer, *Portrait of a Young Girl*, c. 1946 (cat. no. 49)

44. Richard Seewald
German (1889-1976)
Young Girl with Cat (Mädchen mit Katze), 1917
Watercolor on paper
9 5/8 x 7 1/2 in.
Collection of Marvin and Janet Fishman, Milwaukee

Provenance: Galerie Wolfgang Ketterer, Munich

45. Gerrit Sinclair
American (1890-1955)
On the Beach
Oil on board
12 x 9 in.
Collection of Dr. and Mrs. Milton F. Gutglass, Milwaukee

46. Alice Sommer
German (1898-1982)
Two Sisters (Zwei Schwestern), 1925
Pencil on toned paper
25 3/16 x 19 in.
Collection of Marvin and Janet Fishman, Milwaukee

Provenance: Estate of the artist, Dresden; Galerie Saxonia, Munich; Galerie Brockstedt, Hamburg
Exhibitions: Dresdner Kunstgenossenschaft, Annual Exhibition, 1925?; Milwaukee Art Museum, *From Expressionism to Resistance: Art in Germany 1909-1936—The Marvin and Janet Fishman Collection*, 6 December 1990-3 February 1991 (traveled to Berlin, Berlinische Galerie; Frankfurt, Schirn Kunsthalle; Emden, Kunsthalle Emden; New York, The Jewish Museum; Omaha, Joslyn Art Museum; and Atlanta, High Museum), cat. no. 146, illus. p. 127; Stockholm, Liljevalchs Konsthall, *Konst Som Motstånd: Samling Marvin och Janet Fishman*, 18 November 1995-7 January 1996 (traveled to The Hague, Geementemuseum and Paleis Lange Voorhout; Helsinki, Helsingen Taidehalli; and Brussels, Palais de Beaux-Arts), cat. no. 151, illus. p. 148

47. Joaquín Sorolla y Bastida
Spanish (1863-1923)
Drawing in the Sand, c. 1911
Oil on canvas
21 x 25 1/4 in.
Milwaukee Art Museum, Gift of the Samuel O. Buckner Collection, M1919.30

Provenance: Purchased by 1911 (through William E. B. Starkweather?)

48. Chaim Soutine
Lithuanian (1894-1943)
Children and Geese, 1934
Oil on canvas
21 5/8 x 18 1/8 in.
Milwaukee Art Museum, Gift of Mrs. Harry Lynde Bradley, M1959.375

Provenance: Collection of the artist; private collection, Switzerland; Fine Arts Associates, New York, sold 1952
Exhibitions: Milwaukee Downer College, 12 September-24 October 1954; Milwaukee, Jewish Community Center, *Twentieth-Century Art*, 30 January-20 February 1955; Milwaukee Art Center, Bradley Collection, 1 February-4 March 1962; Milwaukee Art Center, *The Collection of Mrs. Harry Lynde Bradley*, 25 October 1968-23 February 1969, cat. no. 69, illus. p. 74; Madison, Elvehjem Art Center, University of Wisconsin, *Inaugural Exhibition: Nineteenth- and Twentieth-Century Art from the Collections of Alumni and Friends*, 11 September-8 November 1970, cat. no. 64, illus. p. 66; Dallas, Northwood Institute, *Selections from the Collection of Mrs. Harry Lynde Bradley*, 21 March-30 April 1971, no. 32 on list; Omaha, Joslyn Art Museum, *The Thirties Decade*, 10 October-28 November 1971, cat. no. 180; Chicago, Spertus Museum of Judaica, *The French Connection: Jewish Artists in the School of Paris, 1900-1940; Works in Chicago Collections*, 24 October-31 December 1982, cat. no. 63, illus.; Milwaukee Art Museum, *The Jewish Contribution in Twentieth-Century Art: Selections from the Permanent Collection*, 19 November 1993-9 January 1994; Tokyo, Isetan Museum of Art, *Twentieth-Century Masters from the Milwaukee Art Museum*, 2 July-9 August 1994 (traveled to Nagoya, Matsuzakaya Art Museum; Asahikawa, Hokkaido Asahikawa Museum of Art; Umeda-Osaka, Daimaru Museum; Chiba, Chiba Sogo Museum of Art; Marugame, Marugame Genichiro-Inokuma Museum of Contemporary Art), cat. no. 26, pp. 62, 137, illus. p. 63
Literature: *Personal Selections from the Collection of Mrs. Harry Lynde Bradley* (New Orleans: The Bradley Family Foundation, Inc., 1975), illus. p. 47

49. Raphael Soyer
American (1899-1987)
Portrait of a Young Girl, c. 1946
Oil on canvas
59 x 29 in.
Collection of Rosenthal and Rosenthal, Inc., New York

Provenance: Dr. Arnold Lieber

50. John Mix Stanley
American (1814-1872)
Young Chief Uncas
Oil on canvas
24 x 20 in.
Autry Museum of Western Heritage, Los Angeles

51. James (Jacques-Joseph) Tissot
French (1836-1902)
The Widower (Le veuf), 1877
Etching and drypoint
13 7/8 x 9 in.
Collection of Dr. and Mrs. Milton F. Gutglass, Milwaukee

Literature: Michael Justin Wentworth, *James Tissot: Catalogue Raisonné of His Prints* (Minneapolis: The Minneapolis Institute of Arts, 1978), no. 28, p. 130, illus. p. 131

52. James (Jacques-Joseph) Tissot
French (1836-1902)
The Garden Bench (Le banc de jardin), 1883
Mezzotint
16 3/8 x 22 3/8 in.
Collection of Dr. and Mrs. Milton F. Gutglass, Milwaukee

Literature: Michael Justin Wentworth, *James Tissot: Catalogue Raisonné of His Prints* (Minneapolis: The Minneapolis Institute of Arts, 1978), no. 75, pp. 290-2, illus. p. 291

53. Jacques Villon (Gaston Duchamp)
French (1875-1963)
Maternity (Maternité), c. 1948
Oil on canvas
57 3/8 x 38 in.
Haggerty Museum of Art,
Gift of Mr. and Mrs. Ira Haupt
62.7

Provenance: Galerie Louis Carré, 1948; Mr. and Mrs. Ira Haupt; their gift to Marquette University, 1962
Literature: Dora Vallier, *Jacques Villon: Oeuvres de 1897 à 1956* (Paris, 1957), p. 90; *Mother and Child in Modern Art*, exh. cat. (New York: American Federation of Arts, 1963), cat. no. 20, illus.; *Selected Works* (Milwaukee: Patrick and Beatrice Haggerty Museum of Art, Marquette University, 1984), pp. 76-77, illus. p. 76

54. Karl Völker
German (1889-1962)
Gypsy Family, c. 1920
Oil on canvas
47 1/2 x 29 1/3 in.
Collection of Marvin and Janet Fishman, Milwaukee

Provenance: Emilio Bertonati; Galerie del Levante, Milan and Munich

55. Édouard Vuillard
French (1868-1940)
Child with Ribbons (Enfant aux rubans), c. 1904-05
Oil on canvas
17 1/2 x 22 1/5 in
Collection of Catherine and David A. Straz, Jr., Milwaukee

Provenance: Acquired from the artist by Jacques Roussel, Paris; Wildenstein & Co., Inc., New York; sold 13 May 1997
Exhibition: Hong Kong, Mandarin Oriental Hotel, *French Impressionists, Post-Impressionists and Their Precursors* (presented by Wildenstein), 5-10 November 1993, illus.
Literature: G. Groom, *Édouard Vuillard, Painter-Decorator* (New Haven and London, 1993), pp. 198-99, illus. fig. 320a; forthcoming catalogue raisonné of the works of Vuillard by Antoine Salomon

56. Andrew W. Warren
American (active 1854-1873)
Clay Modeling, c. 1866
Oil on canvas
10 1/4 x 8 1/4 in.
Collection of Edward Wilson,
Fund for Fine Arts, Chevy Chase, Maryland

57. Frederick Judd Waugh
American (1861-1940)
The Artist's Family at Home, 1887
Oil on canvas
25 x 30 in.
Collection of Mr. and Mrs. Ted Slavin, Los Angeles

Provenance: Hirschl and Adler Galleries, New York

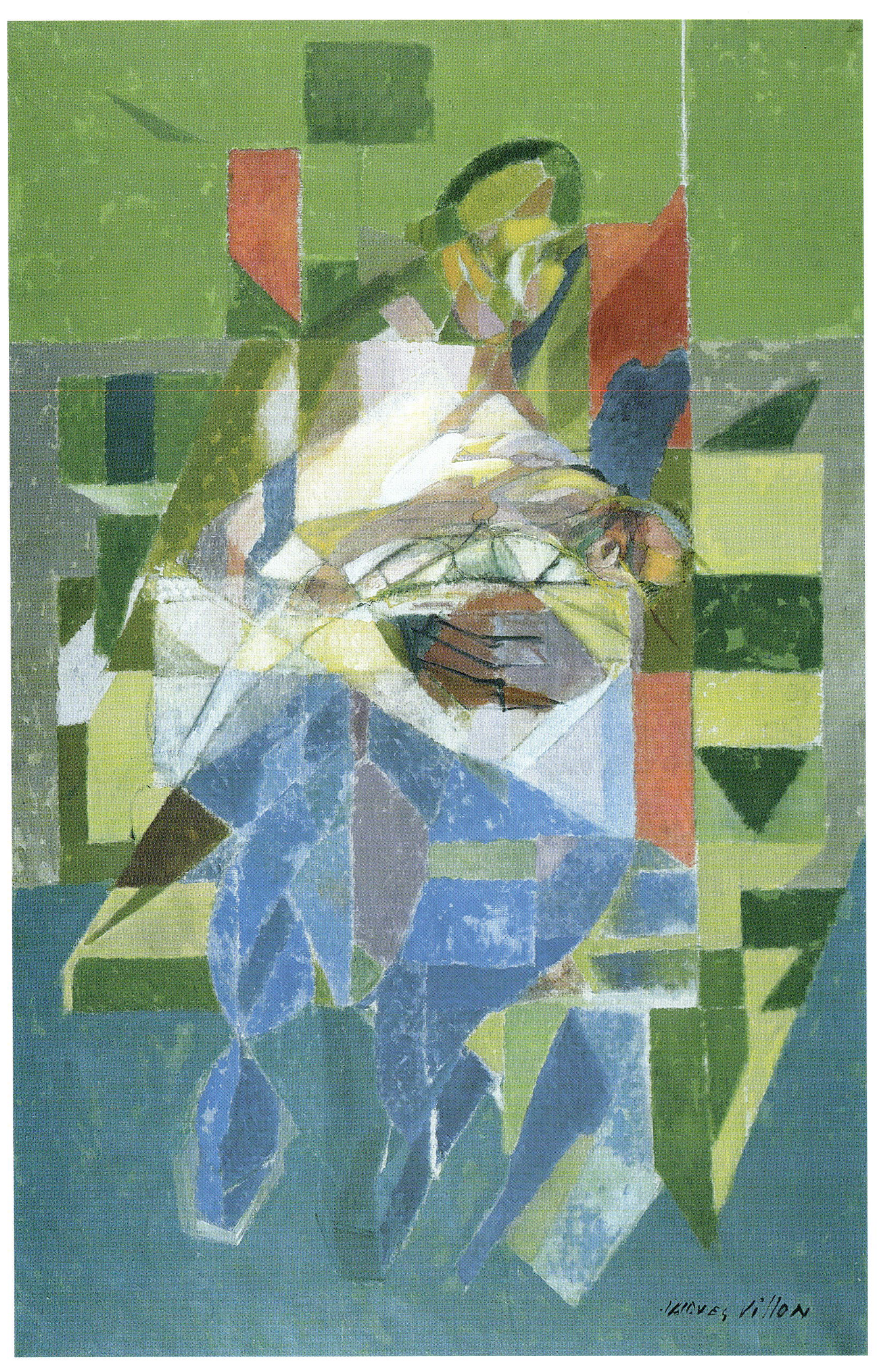

Jacques Villon, *Maternity (Maternité)*, c. 1948 (cat. no. 53)